# Human Rights: Dynamics in India

Prof S Narayan

KALPAZ

ISBN: 978-93-5128-131-3

Price: ₹ 950

First Published, 2015

*Published by,*

Kalpaz Publications
C-30, Satyawati Nagar,
Delhi-110052
Ph. : 9212142040
E-mail: kalpaz@hotmail.com

*Printed at:* G. Print Process, Delhi
Cataloging in Publication Data--DK

Courtesy: D.K. Agencies (P) Ltd. <docinfo@dkagencies.com>

Narayan, S., author.
Dynamics of human rights in India / Prof. S. Narayan.
pages cm
ISBN 9789351281313
1. Human rights--India. I. Title.

KNS2095.N37 2015 DDC 342.54085 23

# Contents

# *Preface*

Human rights in India is well known subject in academic circle but common man is yet to be made aware of the human rights properly. It has been observed that almost 90 percent of population of rural India and 99 percent population of tribal India and almost 50 percent of cosmopolitan cities are unaware of human rights. Generally, jail and police are considered to be the subject of human rights but in the growing and developing India, the umbrella of human rights is also growing health, education, media communication, almost all sphere of life is now under the umbrella of human rights. Along the growing subject of developing country, it becomes our responsibility to educate to common man of India about human rights. In the line, A humble effort is made in this book.

I am thankful to my wife Mrs Shobha Narayan, Children, Dr Shiwani, Prakash, Sri Subhash, Dr Savidhi-Ajeet and Bhamini, Prakhar, Chutri. I am thankful Mr Rohit and Mr Vikash for their valuable help all the while. Thanks to Gyan publishers for their ardent appraisal vide publishing this book.

**Prof S Narayan**
**(Emeritus Professor)**

# Introduction

On 12th October 1993 The Protection of Human Rights Act, 1993 was enacted in India and the commission named National Humans Rights Commission was established on this day. Human Rights flow from the very fact of being born as a human being. They are essentially distinguished from other rights in as much as their violation in any way damages almost irreversibly the sub-liminal process that goes to make up a total, ideal, human being. They lend dignity to the human being. Human rights are sacred, therefore, any event construing to violate it in any manner has to necessarily be of concern to every civilised human being.

The commission has been established in line with the Paris Principal. The National Human Rights Commission (NHRC) of India is an autonomous body constituted by the Centre Government to protect human rights in India under The Protection of Human Rights Act (PHRA) of 1993. The PHRA mandates that "The Central Government shall constitute a body to be known as the National Human Rights Commission to exercise the powers conferred upon, and to perform the function assigned to it, under this Act, "namely protecting the rights relating to life, liberty, equality and dignity of the individual guaranteed by the Constitution and enforceable by Court of India."

The latest Amendment Bill 2006 to Protection of Human Rights Act widens the scope of the functioning of the Commission. It enlarges the definition of Human Rights but substituting that 'International Covenants' viz. ICCPR and ICESCR and such other Covenant or Conventions adopted by the General Assembly of the United Nations, jails or other institutions under the control of state Government can be inspected and supervised without the requirement of prior intimation, thus it enabler surprise visit and empowers NHRC to study the living conditions of the inmates and make recommendations thereon to the Government. The Bill also enlarges the scope of the Commission that wherever the Commission considers it necessary or expedient so to do, it may, by order, transfer any complaint filed or pending before it to the State Human Rights Commission who has jurisdiction to entertain the same.

The statute under which NHRC was established is The Protection of Human Rights Act (PHRA), 1993 as amended by The Protection of Human Rights (Amendment) Act, 2006.

It is in conformity with the 'Paris Principal', adopted at the first international workshop on national institutions for the promotion and protection of human rights held in Paris in October 1991, and endorsed by the General Assembly of the United Nations by its Resolution 48/134 of 20th of December, 1993.

The NHRC is an embodiment of India's concern for the promotion and protection of Human Rights.

Section 2 (1) (d) of the PHRA defines 'Human Rights' as the rights relating to life, liberty, equality and dignity of the individual guaranteed by the International Covenants and enforceable by Court of India.

The 'International Covenants', as per section 2 (1) (f), means the International Covenants of Civil and Political Rights, Economic, Social and Cultural Rights adopted by the General Assembly of the United Nations on 16 December, 1966 and such other Covenants or Conventions adopted by the General Assedmbly of the United Nations as the centre Government may, by notification, specify.

Historically, since the days of the Indus Valley Civilisation, Indian culture has been the product of a synthesis of diverse cultures and religions that came into contact with the enormous Indian sub-continent over a very long stretch of time. As Jawaharlal Nehru notes, there is "an unbroken continuity between the most modern and the most ancient phases of Hindu thought extending over three thousand years." The rights of man have been the concern of all civilisations from time immemorial. "The concept of the rights of man and other fundamental rights was not unknown to the people of earlier periods." The Babylonian laws and the Assyrian laws in the Middle East, the *'Dharma'* of the Vedic period in India and the jurisprudence of Lao-Tze and Confucius in China, have championed human rights throughout the history of human civilisation. The Indian concept perceives the individual, the society and the universe as an organic whole. Everyone is a child of God and all fellow beings are related to one another and belong to a universal family.

Human rights in India is an issue complicated by the country's large size, its tremendous diversity, its status as a developing country and a sovereign, secular, democratic republic. The

Constitution of India provides for fundamental rights, which include freedom of religion. The Articles and Clauses also provide for freedom of speech, as well as separation of executive and judiciary and freedom of movement within the country and abroad. In its report on human rights in India during 2010, Human Rights Watch stated India had 'significant human rights problems'. They identified lack of accountability for security forces and impunity for abusive policing including 'police brutality, extrajudicial killings, and torture' as major problems. In 2011, Margaret Sekaggya, the U.N. Special Rapporteur on the situation of human rights defenders, expressed concern that she found human rights workers and their families who 'have been killed, tortured, ill-treated, disappeared, threatened, arbitrarily arrested and detained, falsely charged and under surveillance because of their legitimate work in upholding human rights and fundamental freedoms. In the forth coming pages I have discussed these all.

# 1

# *Chronology Human Rights Development in India*

1829: The practice of *sati* was formally abolished by Governor General William Benting after years of campaigning by Hindu reform movements such as the Brahmo Samaj of Raja Ram Mohan Roy against this orthodox Hindu funeral custom of self-immolation of widows after the death of their husbands.

1929: Child Marriage Restraint Act, prohibiting marriage of minors under 14 years of age is passed.

1947: India achieves political independence from the British *Raj*.

1950: The Constitution of India establishes a sovereign democratic republic with universal adult franchise. Part 3 of the Constitution contains a Bill of Fundamental Rights enforceable by the Supreme Court and the High Courts. It also provides for reservations for previously disadvantaged sections in education, employment and political representation.

1952: Criminal Tribes Acts repealed by government, former 'criminal tribes' categorised as 'denotified', and Habitual Offenders Act (1952) enacted.

1955: Reform of family law concerning Hindus gives more rights to Hindu women.

1958: Armed Forces (Special Powers) Act, 1958.[3]

1973: Supreme Court of India rules in *Kesavananda Bharati case* that the basic structure of the Constitution (including many fundamental rights) is unalterable by a constitutional amendment.

1975-77: State of Emergency in India extensive rights violations take place.

1978: SC rules in *Menaka Gandhi v. Union of India* that the right to life under Article 21 of the Constitution cannot be suspended even in an emergency.

1978: Jammu and Kashmir Public Safety Act, 1978.

1984: Operation Blue Star, and the subsequent 1984 Anti-Sikh riots.

1984: 2006 Extrajudicial disappearances in Punjab by, caused the police.

1985-86: The *Shah Bano case,* where the Supreme Court recognised the Muslim woman's right to maintenance upon divorce, sparks protests from Muslim clergy. To nullify the decision of the Supreme Court, the Rajiv Gandhi government enacted The Muslim Women (Protection of Rights on Divorce) Act, 1986.

1987: *Hashimpura massacre* during communal riots in Meerut.

1989: Scheduled Caste and Scheduled Tribe (Prevention of Atrocities) Act, 1989 is passed.

1989: Kashmiri insurgency sees ethnic cleansing of Kashmere *Pandits,* desecrating Hindu temples, killing of Hindus and Sikhs, and abductions of foreign tourists and government functionaries.

1992: A constitutional amendment establishes Local Self-Government (Panchayati Raj) as a third tier of governance at the village level, with one-third of the seats reserved for women. Reservations were provided for scheduled castes and tribes as well.

1992: Babri Masjid demolished by mobs, resulting in riots across the country.

1993: National Human Rights Commission is established under the Protection of Human Rights Act.

2001: Supreme Court passes extensive orders to implement the right to food.[6]

2002: Violence in Gujarat, chiefly targeting its minority, claims many lives.

2005: A powerful Right to Information Act is passed to give citizen's access to information held by public authorities.[7]

2005: National Rural Employment Guarantee Act (NREGA) guarantees universal right to employment.

2005: Disappearance of Jaswant Singh Khalra by the Punjab Police (Khalra brought to light the extrajudicial disappearances in Punjab).

2006: Supreme Court orders police reforms in response to the poor human rights record of Indian police.

2009: Delhi High Court declares that Section 377 of the Indian Penal Code, which outlaws a range of unspecified 'unnatural' sexual acts, is unconstitutional when applied to homosexual acts between private consenting individuals, effectively decriminalising homosexual relationships in India.

Human Rights are the fundamental rights of the people of India. Section 2 (i) of The Protection of Human Rights Association defines 'Human Rights' as the rights relating to life, liberty, equality and dignity of the individual guaranteed by the constitution or embodied in the International Covenants and enforceable by courts in India.

The 'International Covenants', as per section 2 (i) (f) means the "international covenants" on civil and political rights economic, social and cultural rights adopted by the General Assembly of the United Nations on 16 December, 1966, and such other covenants or conventions adopted by the general assembly of the United Nations as the Central Government may, by notification, specify.

**Pic. 1.1**

Justice K.G. Bala Krishnan, Former Chief Justice of India and chairperson of National Human Rights Commission has mentioned in his foreword of *Achievements of NHRC, Vol.-1,* published in 2012 that "Human Rights flow from the very fact of being born a human being. They are essentially distinguished from other rights in as much as their violation in any way, damages almost irreversibly the subliminal process that go to make up a total, ideal, human being. They lend dignity to the human form. Human Rights are sacred; therefore any court even construing to violate it in any manner has to necessarily be of concern to every civilised human being."

I have mentioned in one of my book that the Human Rights empower an individual to lead life with dignity. In one of my book

*'Anthropology of Disaster Management'* (Gyan Publishers, 2000, page. 16) have written that power is the ability to do something; strength, force, vigor, energy, ability to control or influence others, ability to impose one's will. Thereby empowerment means inducing all these characteristics in an individual. Thus, empowerment is an ability to control or influence or make the people willing for the development which may be economic, social, cultural or political and thereby raising the level of human rights of the individual.

The various forms of power act and interact on each other so significantly, that if the study of power were confined to a single aspect much would be lost in the understanding of the overall dynamics of the system.

It is perhaps in social system that the concept of power is most important. One of the great problems in constructing the general theory of power is the taxonomic difficulties. The very word 'power' is used in variety of ways. In source system and human behavior, there is a larger concept of power; to what extent and how we can get what we want? There are three broad categories of power: threat power, economic power and integrative power. Human rights come under integrative power. Integrative power is the concern of the anthropologists although it has not been studied very explicitly.

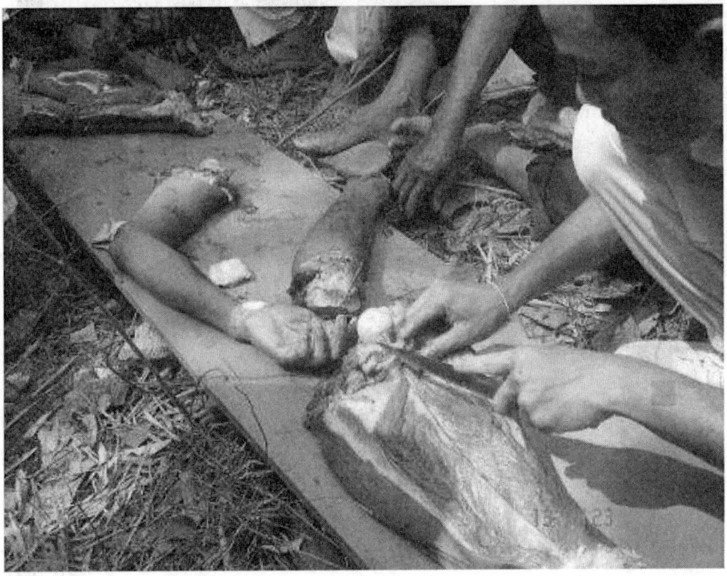

**Pic. 1.2**

It is the dominant power that is the most dominant and significant form of power, in the sense that neither threat power, nor economic power can achieve very much in the absence of legitimacy, which is one of the most important aspects of integrative power. Without legitimacy, both threat and riches are the great fallacies especially of political thinking in regard to power, is to elevate threat power to the position of dominance which it does not really possess. Failure to understand this is an enormous source of error in human decisions, both at the individual level of those who control organisation, and at the group level which gets reflected in social control. Human rights are the ways of mechanism of social control.

**Pic. 1.3**

Thus, it is clear; the empowerment through human rights is the most elusive. Empowerment with reference to human rights means providing systematic development inputs to the target group. It is achieved through a continuous, systematic and scientific process. It is a part of the planning process for the development of mankind.

While planning for the development of the target group, the desired development is expected through empowerment inputs.

It has been found in one of my earlier studies that higher the development inputs—higher the exploitation and higher the exploitation led to:-

- Deprivatory Human Rights,
- Discriminatory Human Rights, and
- Differential Human Rights.

In the preface of my book *Sustainable Development (Common Wealth-2005 p.v)* have written that "Anthropologists have great concern for development as well as sustainable development and human developments. This may be, probably, the reason that international institutions lay emphasis on recruitment of anthropologists for execution and evolution of development programmes. The anthropologist are considered to be an expert of giving human face and human touch to development inputs, programmes and polices"; it stands true with reference to human rights.

Development is not in abstract but is in reality and visible. Many development policies and programmes are being drafted and executive but the 'N' product it is the Myopic Economic Development indicators with statistical jargons. Higher the Myopic Economic Developments, higher the violation of human rights.

**Pic. 1.4**

## Use of Torture by Police

The Asian Centre for Human Rights estimated that from 2002 to 2008, over four people per day died in police custody, with 'hundreds' of those deaths were caused due to police use of torture. According to a report written by the Institute of Correctional Administration (Punjab), up to 50 per cent of police officers in the country have used physical or mental abuse on prisoners. Instances of torture, such as through lack of sanitation, space, or water have been documented in West Bengal as well.

## Other violence

Conflicts such as Anti-Bihari sentiment have sometimes escalated to violance. Invasive methods like 'microanalysis' (controlled anesthesia) are now commonly permitted by Indian courts for crime investigation. Even though according to Indian constitution "nobody may be made a witness against himself", courts have recently proclaimed that even permission from court is not necessary for conducting this practice. 'Narcoanalysis' is now widely used to replace/circumvent the lack of skill and infrastructure for conducting scientific methods of crime investigation. 'Marcoanalysis' is also alleged as against medical ethics.

**Pic. 1.5**

It has been found that more than half of the prisoners of the country are detained without adequate evidence. Unlike in other democratic countries, the investigation in India generally commence with the arrest of the accused. As the judicial system is understaffed and sluggish, it is not uncommon to find innocent civilians languishing in jail for many years. For instance, the Bombay High Court in September 2009 asked the Maharashtra government to pay ₹ 100,000 as compensation to a 40-year-old man who languished in prison for over 10 years for a crime he didn't commit.

**Pic. 1.6**

## Aims of the Study

The present study aims:

1. To provide basic data on unilinear or multilinear human rights, horizontal or vertical human rights to each citizen in India;
2. To suggest steps and measures for unilinear human rights to each citizen in India.

Methodology:
Data collected from Chhattisgarh, Madhya Pradesh and Jharkhand are analysed and may be focussed in national perspective.

The sample size are from different age groups and from both sex groups, and from all professional groups beginning from labourer to politician. After data collection, it was tabulated and analysed and finally book is before you; research techniques of data collection of social science were used for data collection, tabulation and analysis and report.

# 2

# *Human Rights and the Indian Constitution*

The Constitution of the Republic of India which came into force on 26th January, 1950 with 395 Articles and 8 Schedules is one of the most elaborate fundamental laws ever adopted. The Preamble to the Constitution declares India to be a sovereign, socialist, secular and democratic republic. The term 'democratic' denotes that the Government gets its authority from the will of the people. It gives a feeling that they all are equal "irrespective of the race, religion, language, sex and culture." The Preamble to the Constitution lays emphasis on justice; social, economic and political, liberty of thought, expression, belief, faith and worship, equality of status and of opportunity and fraternity assuring the dignity of the individual, and the unity and integrity of the nation to all its citizens.

## India and the Universal Declaration

India was a signatory to the Universal Declaration of Human Rights. A number of fundamental rights guaranteed for the individuals in Part III of the Indian constitution are similar to the provisions of the Universal Declaration of Human Rights. The following table makes it very clear.

**Pic. 2.1**

**Table 2.1** Civil and Political Rights in the Universal Declaration of Human Rights and in the Indian Constitution

| *S.No.* | *Name of Rights* | *Universal Declaration* | *Indian Constitution* |
|---|---|---|---|
| 1. | Equality before law | Article 7 | Article 14 |
| 2. | Prohibition of discrimination | Article 7 | Article 15(1) |
| 3. | Equality of opportunity | Article 21 (2) | Article 16(1) |

*Continued*

| | | | |
|---|---|---|---|
| 4. | Freedom of speech and expression | Article 19 | Article 19(l) (a) |
| 5. | Freedom of peaceful assembly | Article 20(1) | Article 19(1) (b) |
| 6. | Right to form associations or unions | Article 23(4) | Article 19(1) (c) |
| 7. | Freedom of movement within the border | Article 13 (1 ) | Article 19(1) (d) |
| 8. | Protection in respect of conviction for offences | Article 11 (2) | Article 20 (1) |
| 9. | Protection of life and personal liberty | Article 3 | Article 21 |
| 10. | Protections of slavery and forced labour | Article 4 | Article 23 |
| 11. | Freedom of conscience and religion | Article 18 | Article 25(1 |
| 12. | Remedy for enforcement of rights | Article 8 | Article 32 |
| 13. | Right against arbitrary arrest and detention | Article 9 | Article 22 |
| 14. | Right to social security | Article 22 | Article 29(1) |

The Table below shows that most of the economic, social and cultural rights proclaimed in the Universal Declaration of Human Rights have been incorporated in part IV of the Indian Constitution.

**Table 2.2** **Economic, Social and Cultural Rights in the Universal Declaration of Human Rights and in the Indian Constitution**

| *S.No.* | *Name of Rights* | *Universal Declaration* | *Indian Constitution* |
|---|---|---|---|
| 1. | Right to work, to just and *eavorable* conditions of work | Article 23 (1) | Article 41 |
| 2. | Right to justice against exploitation and remuneration | Article 23(3) | Article 43 |
| 3. | Right to arrest and detention right to education | Article 26(1) | Articles 21 (A), 41,45 & 51A(k) |
| 4. | Right of everyone to a standard of living for him and his family | Article 25(1) | Article 39(a) & Article 47 |
| 5. | Right to a proper social order | Article 28 | Article 38 |

*In Keshavananda Bharti v. State of Kerala,* the Supreme Court observed, "The Universal Declaration of Human Rights may not be a legally binding instrument but it shows how India understood the nature of human rights at the time the Constitution was adopted." In the case of *Jolly George Varghese v. bank of Cochin,* the point involved was whether a right incorporated in the Covenant on Civil and Political Rights, which is not recognised in the Indian Constitution, shall be available to the individuals in India? Justice Krishna Iyer reiterated dualism and asserted that the positive commitment of the State parties ignites legislative action at home but does not automatically make the Covenant an enforceable part of the *corpus juries* in India. Thus, although the Supreme Court has stated that the Universal Declaration cannot create a binding set of rules and that even international treaties may at best inform judicial institutions and inspire legislative action. Constitutional interpretation in India has been strongly influenced by the Declara-

**Pic. 2.2**

tion. In the judgment given in *Chairman, Railway Board others* V. Chandrima, Supreme Court, observed that the Declaration has the international recognition as the moral code of conduct having been adopted by the general assembly of the United Nations. The applicability of the Universal Declaration of Human Rights and principles thereof may have to be read, if need be, into the domestic jurisprudence. In a number of cases the declaration has been referred to in the decisions of the Supreme Court and State high courts. India ratified the International Covenant on Civil and Political Rights and the International Covenant on Economic, Social and Cultural Rights on March 27, 1979. The Optional Protocol to the International Covenant on Civil and Political Rights, 1989, however, was not ratified by India.

## The Constitutional and Institutional Framework of Human Rights in India. Fundamental Rights and Human Rights

The judicially enforced fundamental rights encompass all seminal civil and political rights and some of the rights of minorities' arena enshrined in part III of the Constitution (Articles 12-35). These include the rights to equality, the right to freedom, the right against exploitation, the right to freedom of religion, cultural, educational rights and the right to constitutional remedies. Fundamental rights differ from ordinary rights in the sense that the former are inviolable. No law, ordinance, custom, usage, or administrative order can abridge or take them away. Any law, which is violative of any of the fundamental rights, is void. In *ADM Jabalpur v. Shukla,* Justice Beg observed, "The object of making certain general aspects of rights fundamental is to guarantee them against illegal invasion of these rights by executive, legislative, or judicial organ of the State." Earlier, Chief Justice Subba Rao in *Golak Nath v. State of Punjab* had rightly observed, "Fundamental rights are the modern name for what have been traditionally known as natural rights."

The Supreme Court of India recognises these fundamental rights as 'Natural Rights' or 'Human Rights'. While referring to the fundamental rights contained in part III of the Constitution, Justice Sikri the then Chief Justice of India, in *Keshavananda Bharati v. State of Kerala,* observed, "I am unable to hold these provisions to show that rights are not natural or inalienable rights. As a matter of fact India was a party to the Universal Declaration of Rights and that Declaration describes some fundamental rights as inalienable." The Chief Justice Patanjali Shastri in *State of West Bengal v. Subodh Gopal Gosh* referred to fundamental rights as those great and basic rights, which are recognised and guaranteed as the natural rights inherent in the status of a citizen of a free country Article 14 of the Indian constitution proclaims the general right of all

**Pic. 2.3**

persons to equality before law, while Article 15 prohibits the State from discriminating citizens on grounds of religion, race, caste, sex or place of birth, and prohibits any restriction on any citizen's access to any public place, including wells and tanks. Equality of opportunity for all citizens in matters of public employment is guaranteed under Article 16. Article 17 abolishes untouchability and makes its practice an offence punishable under law. Both Articles 15 and 16 enable the State to make special provisions for the advancement of socially and educationally backward classes, castes and tribes, they as recognised in the Constitution (known as the Scheduled Castes and Scheduled Tribes) require very special treatment for their advancement. Article 18 abolishes all non-military or non-academic titles. The right to freedom guaranteed to all citizens under Article 19 encompasses the right to freedom of speech and expression, the right to assemble peaceably without arms, the right to form associations or unions, the right to move freely throughout the territory of India, the right of residence, and the right to practice any profession, or to carry on any occupation, trade or business. The protection of a person in respect of conviction of offences under Article 20 includes protection against *ex post facto* criminal laws, the principle of *outré* force convict and the right against self-incrimination. Article 21, is core of all fundamental rights provisions in the Indian constitution, ordains: "No person shall be deprived of his life or personal liberty except according to procedure established by law."

Article 21A was added to the Constitution by the Eighty Sixth Constitutional Amendment Acts, 2002. Article 21A proclaims, "The State shall provide free and compulsory education to all children of the age of six to fourteen years in such manner as the State may, by law, determine." The rights of a person, arrested and detained by the State authorities, are provided in Article 22. These include the right to be informed of the grounds of arrest, the right to legal advice and the right to be produced before a magistrate within 24 hours of arrest (except where one is arrested under a preventive detention law). The right against exploitation includes prohibition of trafficking in human beings and forced labour (Article 23), and prohibition of employment of children below 14 years of age "to work in any factory or mine or in any other hazardous employment." Subject to public order and morality, all persons are equally entitled to freedom of conscience and the right to profess, practise and propagate religion (Article 25). Every religious denomination or section also has the right to establish and maintain religious institutions and manage their religious affairs (Article 26). No one may be compelled to pay

Pic. 2.4

**Table 2.3 Different Articles of the International Covenant on Civil and Political Rights and the Indian Constitution**

| No. | Name of Rights | Covenant on Civil and Political Rights | Indian Constitution |
|---|---|---|---|
| 1. | Forced labour | Article 8(3) | Article 23 |
| 2. | Equality before law | Article 14(1) | Article 14 |
| 3. | Prohibition of discrimination | Article 26 | Article 15 |
| 4. | Equality of opportunity to public service | Article 25(C) | Article 16(1) |
| 5. | Freedom of speech and expression | Article 19(1) and (2) | Article 19(1) (a) |
| 6. | Right for peaceful assembly | Article 21 | Article 19(1) (b) |
| 7. | Right to freedom of association | Article 22(1) | Article 19(1) (c) |
| 8. | Right to move freely within the territory of a state | Article 12(1) | Article 19(1) (d) |
| 9. | Protection is respect of conviction of offences | Article 15(1) | Article 20(1) |
| 10. | Protection from prosecution and punishment | Article 14(7) | Article 20(2) |
| 11. | Not to be compelled testify against himself | Article 14(3)(g) | Article 20(3) |
| 12. | Right to life and liberty | Article 6(1) and 9(1) | Article 21 |
| 13. | Right to child education | Article 26(1) | Article 21(A) |
| 14. | Protection against arrest and detention | Article 9(2)(3) and (4) | Article 22 |
| 15. | Freedom of conscience and religion | Article 18(1) | Article 25 |

any religious taxes (Article 27). The wholly state-funded educational institutions are barred from imparting religious instructions (Article 28). The rights of any section of citizens or a minority to promote its distinct language, script or culture, to have access to State-funded educational institutions (Article 29), and to establish and maintain educational institutions of its choice (Article 30) are also guaranteed. The right to Constitution meaning is essentially the right to move the Supreme Court of India for enforcement of the above rights (Article 32). The Supreme Court is vested with wide constitutional powers in this regard. They include the power to issue directions, orders or writs for the enforcement of the fundamental rights (Article 32(2)). State (i.e. provincial) High Courts, too, have identical powers (Article 226). As laws inconsistent with or in derogation of the rights conferred by part III of the Constitution are void (Article 13), the courts having the power to adjudge the constitutional validity of all laws. Furthermore, by virtue of Article 141, the law declared by the Supreme Court shall be binding on all courts in India. Fundamental rights guaranteed under the Indian constitution may be divided, for the sake of convenience, into two categories, *viz.,* specified fundamental rights and other fundamental rights (rights not specifically enumerated).

### Specified Fundamental Rights

Many rights enshrined in the Covenant on Civil and Political Rights have been recognised specially in the Indian constitution as 'fundamental rights.' They may be referred to as 'specified' fundamental rights because they are mentioned in the Constitution by name.

### Fundamental Rights for Citizens Only

The Indian constitution has classified fundamental rights into two categories: (1) fundamental rights which are available to citizens only; (2) fundamental rights available to all persons residing within the territory of India for the time being and subjected to its jurisdiction. The first of the category, which is available to the citizens includes the following articles:

### Articles

(1). Article 15 relating to prohibition of discrimination on grounds of religion, race, caste, sex or place of birth.

(2). Article 16 relating to equality of opportunity for all citizens in matters of public appointment.

(3). Article 19 relating to protection of rights:

- (a). Freedom of speech and expression.
- (b). To assemble peaceably and without arms.
- (c). To form associations or unions.
- (d). To move freely throughout the territory of India.
- (e). To reside and settle in any part of the territory of India.
- (f). Article 19(1) (f) relating to the right to own and acquire property was deleted by the Constitution 42" Amendment Act 1978 with effect from 20-06-1979 g) To prac-

tice any profession or to carry on any occupation, trade or business'.

(4). Article 29 relating to protection of interests of minorities

The second category of fundamental rights comprises the remaining fundamental rights which use the word 'person.' In *Hans Muller of Nurenburg v. Superintendent Presidency Jail Kolkata* was laid down in the judgment that Article 19 applies only to citizens. Fundamental rights mentioned in Article 19, which contains the right to 'basic freedoms', are available only to the citizens of the country. The word 'citizen' that occurs in the above article has not been used in a sense different from that in which it has been used in part II of the Constitution dealing with citizenship.

In *Anwar v. State of Jammu and Kashmir,* it was held that non-citizens could not claim fundamental rights provided under Article 19. In *Chairman, Railway Board and others v. Chandrima,* the Supreme Court has observed that fundamental rights are available to all the persons of this country and those who are not citizens of this country and who come here as tourists or in any other capacity are entitled to the protection of their lives in accordance with the constitutional provisions. They also have a right to life in this country. Thus, they also have the right to live with human dignity so long as they are here in India. Article 14 which guarantees equality before law and equal protection of laws within the territory of India is applicable to 'person' who would also include both the 'citizens' of this country and non-citizens. In this case, a Bangladeshi national Mrs Khatoon was gang raped by the railway employees in a room at the Yatri Niwas of the Howrah railway station in West Bengal. The Calcutta High Court allowed compensation of a sum of rupees 10 lakhs to her for having been gang raped. Upholding the decision of the High Court, the Supreme Court held that as a national of another country, she could not be subjected to a treatment, which was below the dignity, nor could she be subjected to physical violence at the hands of Government employees who outraged her modesty. Acceeding to the tone and the tenor of the language used in Article 21, they the rights are available not only to every citizen of this country but also to a person of another country. The Apex Court also held that since the word 'life' has been used in Article 21 of the Constitution as a basic human right in the same sense as understood in the Universal Declaration of Human Rights of 1,48, there is no reason why it should be given a narrow meaning.

**Pic. 2.5**

Article 39(a) and Article 44 of the Directive Principles of State Policy contained in part IV of the Constitution are for the citizens only.

### Other Fundamental Rights

A number of rights, which are stated in the Covenant, are not laid down in part Ill of the Constitution. The Indian constitution has specifically enumerated all the fundamental rights. *In Birma v. State of Rajasthan* was held that "Treaties which are part of international law do not form part of the Law of the land, unless explicitly made so by the legislative authority." Further in *Shiv Kumar Sharma and others v. Union of India,* the Delhi High Court held that in India treaties do not have the force of law, and consequently obligations arising therefrom will not be enforceable in municipal law unless backed by legislation. In *A.D.M. Jabalpur v. S. huidtahe,* Supreme Court by a majority of four to one, held that the Constitution of India did not recognise any natural or common law rights other than that expressly conferred in the Constitution. The attitude of the Supreme Court has changed especially after 1978. The courts on many occasions by accepting the rule of judicial construction have held that regard must be paid to international conventions and norms for constructing domestic law. In *Maneka Gandhi v. Union of India,* Justice Bhagwati in the special bench for the Supreme Court observed that the expression 'personal liberty' in Article 21 is of the widest amplitude and it covers a variety of rights, which go to constitute the responsibility of man and some of them have been raised to the status of distinct fundamental rights and given additional protection under Article 19. No person can be deprived of his right to go abroad unless there is a law made by State prescribing the procedure for so depriving him, and the deprivation is effected strictly in accordance with such procedure.

**Pic. 2.6**

The following are the rights contained in the Covenant on Civil and Political Rights. They are available to the citizens of India through judicial decisions, though they are specifically mentioned in the Constitution.

(1). Right to travel abroad (Article 21) is a guaranteed right under Article 12 (2) of the Covenant on Civil and Political Rights. In *Sathwant Singh Sawhney v. D. Ramanathan, assistant passport officer, New Delhi,* the court held that the right to go abroad is part of an individual's personal liberty within the meaning of Article 21.

(2). Right to privacy (Articles 21 and 19 (1) (d)) is stipulated under Article 17 (1) of the Covenant on Civil and Political Rights. In *Kharak Singh v. State of Uttar pradesh,* it was held by the Supreme Court that the domiciliary visits stand in infringement of the right to privacy and is violative of the citizen's fundamental rights of personal liberty guaranteed under Article 21.

(3). Right against solitary confinement;
(4). Right to human dignity;
(5). Right to free legal aid in a criminal trial.
(6). Right to speedy trial.
(7). Right against handcuffing.
(8). Right against delayed execution.
(9). Right against custodial violance.
(10). Right against public hanging.
(11). Right to healthcare or doctor's assistance.
(12). Right to shelter.
(13). Right to pollution-free environment.
(14). Freedom of the press.
(15). Right to know.
(16). Right to compensation.
(17). Right to release and rehabilitation of bonded labour.
(18). Right of inmates of protection homes.
(19). Right of not to be imprisoned for inability to fulfill a contractual obligation. In *Jolly George Varghese v. Bank of Cochin,* it was held by the Supreme Court that to cast a person in prison because of his poverty and subsequent inability to meet his contractual liability is a violation of Article 21.

# 3

# *Human Rights Media and Judiciary*

Judiciary third *a-vis* Human Rights is the three organs of Government. The judiciary has become a vanguard of human rights in India. It performs this function mainly by innovative interpretation and application of the human rights provisions of the Constitution. The Supreme Court of India in the case *Ajay Hasia v. Khalidujidbec* has ordered that it has a special responsibility, "to enlarge the range and meaning of the fundamental rights and to advance the human rights jurisprudence." As has already been pointed out, the Supreme Court of India and the State High Courts have ordered powers under the Constitution to enforce the fundamental rights and they have liberally interpreted these powers. The major contributions of the judiciary to the human rights jurisprudence have been in two fields: (a) the substantive expansion of the concept of human rights under Article 21 of the Constitution, and (b) the procedural innovation of public interest litigation.

**Pic. 3.1**

## Expansion of Article

### Article 21

Article 21 reads as follows:
Protection of Life and Personal Liberty - "No person shall be deprived of his life or personal liberty except according to the procedure established by law."

The expansion of Article 21 of the Constitution has taken place in two respects:

(a). The expression 'the procedure established by law' received a new interpretation not intended by the founding fathers of the Constitution. In 1950, the very first year of the Constitution, the Supreme Court in the case *A.K. Gopalan v. State* reflecting on the intentions of the Constitution-makers, held that 'procedure established by law' only meant that a procedure had to be set by law enacted by a legislature. This phrase was deliberately used in Article 21 in preference to the American 'Due Process' clause. Three decades later, in *Maneka Gandhi v. Union of India case,* the Supreme Court rejected its earlier interpretation and held that the procedure contemplated under Article 21 is a right, just and fair procedure, not an arbitrary or oppressive procedure. The procedure, which is reasonable and fair, must now be in conformity with the test of article 14 "in effect it has become a Due Process." There is no doubt that the experience of National Emergency (1975-1977) prompted the Court to go all out for vindication of human rights. Since then every case of infringement of rights by the legislature has undergone judicial scrutiny in terms of the new interpretation laid down in the *Maneka Gandhis case.* Further, this approach has led to procedural due process innovations, such as the right to claim legal aid for the poor and the right to expeditious trial.

(b). The judiciary interprets 'the right to life and personal liberty' to encompass all basic conditions for a life with dignity and liberty. Such an approach allows it to come down heavily on the system of administration of criminal justice and law enforcement. It also brings into the fold of Article 21 all those directive principles of state policy that are essential for a 'life with dignity.' Thus, the judiciary has interpreted 'life' to include the right to possession of each organ of one's body and a prohibition of torture or inhuman or degrading treatment by police. In the *Francis Cora lie Mullin vs. The Administrator, Union territory of Delhi case,* the Supreme Court held that 'life' couldn't be restricted to mere animal existence, or physical survival. The right to life means the right to live with dignity and all that goes with it the basic necessities of life such as adequate nutrition, clothing, shelter and facilities for reading, writing and expressing oneself. Many of the Article 21 cases that came before the High Courts and the Supreme Court often revealed "a shocking state of affairs and portray a complete lack of concern for human values." In *Hussainara Khatoon v. Home Secretary, Bihar,* it has been held by the Supreme Court that though speedy trial is not specifically enumerated as a fundamental right, it is implicit in the broad sweep and content of Article 21, which deals with the 'right to life and liberty'. Justice Bhagwati held if a person is deprived of his liberty under a procedure which it not 'reasonable', 'fair' or 'just', it would fall foul of Article 21. There can, therefore, be no doubt that speedy trial, and by speedy trial we mean reasonably expeditious trial, is an integral and essential part of the fundamental right to life and liberty enshrined in Article 21. It was also held by the Supreme Court that 'detention in jail for a period longer than what they would have been sentenced for, if convicted, is illegal as being a violation of their fundamental right under Article 21 of the Constitution. *Deoraj Khatri v. State of Bihar* raised the case of police brutality in which 80 suspected criminals were brutally blinded during police investigation (*Bhagalpur blinding case*). The Supreme Court condemned it as a "barbaric act and a crime against mankind." In *Sheela Barse v. The State of Maharashtra,* the court was confronted with the custodial violence against women and it laid down certain guidelines against torture and ill treatment of women in police custody and jails. The Supreme Court has also read into Article 21 a right to monetary compensation for deprivations of the right to life and liberty suffered at the hands of the State. This was highlighted in the *Rudal Shah v. State of Bihar.* The emergence of the right to compensation has nullified one of the reservations made by India in its instrument of accession to the human rights Covenants, which stated that the Indian law did not recognise such a right in the event of right deprivation. The health problems of workers in the asbestos industry led the Supreme Court in the case *Paramanand Katra v. Union of India* to rule that the right to life and liberty under Article 21 also encompasses the right of the workers to health and medical aids. The right to life has been held to include the right to receive instant medical aid in case of injury and the right of a child to receive free education up to the age of fourteen.

## PIL

Public Interest Litigation and Human Rights Public Interest Litigation—an expansion of class action under the common law—is a procedural innovation, which the Indian judiciary has by now fairly perfected on the basis of a concept borrowed from the United States. The rules of normally dictate that he who approaches the court must prove his legal standing *vis-à-vis* the claim he seeks to vindicate, usually in terms of a legal right or a legal obligation violated by the defendants on dent causing thereby some injury or damage to him for which law provides a remedy. On the other hand, the public interest litigation is based on the principle that we cannot write off the weaker victims of injustices; the court's doors when they knock shall open ... How can a bonded labourer working in a stone quarry ever know of moving to the Supreme Court? asks Justice Krishna lyer, a public interest activist judge of the Supreme Court of the seventies. He explains that public interest litigation, chiefly, in the realm of public law assists 'all people concerned with governmental lawlessness, negligence of the administration, environmental pollution, public health, product safety, consumer protection and social exploitation being served by professionals like lawyers and public interest lobbies working for 'reform of decision-making processes in Government and outside, affecting the public at large'. Public Interest Law offers new challenges and opportunities of the committed lawyers and social groups to serve the unequal segments of society better. This sensitive development is part of democracy (of the disabled) and of the movement to vindicate social justice through professions for the people. As a result, 'judges with a vision have new universes to behold, and mansions of people's justice to build.' Justice Krishna lyer realises that the public interest litigation is likely to be abused. Hence, he advised that the court should *prima facie* be satisfied that the information laid before it is of such a nature that it calls for examination. By looking at the credentials of the informant, the specific nature of the allegation, the gravity or seriousness of the complaint, and any other relevant circumstances should also be derived. It should also use its own wide investigative faculties as appropriate for the situation. Ever since the public interest litigation are to be promoted by the Supreme Court, there has been an ongoing debate in the country between its supporters and opponents. In the *Sunil Batra v. Union of India* the Supreme Court entertained a letter from Batra, a prisoner, complaining about the treatment meted out to a fellow prisoner in a jail. The letter activated the court to deal with a wide variety of issues such as solitary confinement in jails, conditions of under-trial prisoners, sexual exploitation, sexual exploitation of blind girls in schools, detention of mentally ill persons, minimum wages, illegal sale of babies, bonded labour, environmental protection, ill-treatment of freshers in colleges, better roads, land entitlement, conditions of children in children's homes, treatment of inmates of care homes, conditions of mental hospitals and deaths at alleged police encounters.

As the court opened its doors wide shedding procedure formalism, many of these issues repeatedly came before it as well as many others such as torture of young prisoners, police brutality like blinding of suspects during investigation, custodial violence against women prisoners, deaths in police custody, handcuffing of accused persons facing trials and fetters on incarcerated prisoners. As the legal procedure became deformalised, the court evolved new devices to assist it in dealing with public interest litigation, such as special inquiry, fact-finding commission, and scheme remedies and post-decisional monitoring. A nation-wide legal aid scheme came to be established on the initiative of the Supreme Court in 1982. The Supreme Court promised to examine a range of relevant issues concerning the public interest litigation procedure. An examination of these issue may be useful to streamline the public interest litigation law and practice with a view to discouraging abuses. As Justice Krishna lyer remarked it is "too late to burke PIL, but always welcome to reaffirm and reference laminate the entropy and abuse of the process." It is quite possible that the burden of a backlog of cases awaiting adjudication is what worries the court. But this is never a reason when 'we the people of India demand social justice' reminds justice.

The judiciary should never bite more than it can chew; Justice Sujata Manohar strikes a note of caution in the context of the Constitution. Article embodies a judicially enforceable right. Therefore, it should essentially be a right capable of being protected by a judicial order. A right not capable of such enforcement if spelled out, may result in the trivialisation of court's pronouncements and may encourage the habit of ignoring them. Every human right may not be capable of judicial tenement. It points out the limits and limitations of judicial activism. Taking into account the peculiar nature of public interest litigation, the Supreme Court of India in public interest litigation, *D.K. Basu v. State of West Bengal* issued guidelines to be followed in all cases for arrest and detention by the State interrogatory agencies till legal provisions are made on that behalf as preventive measures.

**The Guidelines**

(1). The police personnel carrying out the arrest and handling the interrogation of the arrestee should bear accurate, visible and clear identification and name tags with their designations. The particulars of such personnel who handle interrogation of the arrestee must be recorded in a register.

(2). The police officer effecting the arrest shall prepare a memo at the time of arrest and shall be attested by at least one witness. This may be either a member of the family of the arrested or a respectable person of the locality from where the arrest is made. It shall be countersigned by the arrestee and shall contain the time and date of arrest.

(3). A person who has been arrested or detained and is being held in custody in a police station or interrogation centre or other lock-ups, shall be entitled to have one friend or relative or other person known to him or having interest in his welfare being informed as soon as possible that he has been arrested and is being detained in a particular place, unless the attesting witness of the memo of arrest is himself such friend or a relative of the arrestee.

(4). The time, place of arrest and venue of custody of an arrestee must be notified by the police when the next friend or relative of the arrestee lives outside the district or town through the Legal Aid Organisation in the district and the police station of the area concerned by telegraphy always within 8-12 hours of the arrest.

(5). The person arrested must be made aware of his right to have someone informed of his arrest or detention as soon as he is put under arrest or is detained.

(6). An entry must be made in the diary at the place of detention regarding the arrest of the person which shall also disclose the name of the next friend of the person who has been informed of the arrest and the names and particulars of the police officials in whose custody the arrestee is.

(7). The arrestee should, where he so requests, be also examined at the time of his arrest: and the major and minor injuries if any present on his body and must be recorded at that time. The 'memo Inspection of' must be signed by both the arrested and the police officer effecting the arrest and a copy shall be provided to the arrestee.

(8). The arrestee should be subjected to medical examination every 48 hours during his detention custody by a doctor from a panel of approved doctors appointed by the director, health services of the State concerned or Union Territory. He should prepare such a panel for all tehsils and districts as well.

(9). Copies of all the documents including the memo of arrest referred above should be sent to the magistrate for his record.

(10). The arrestee may be permitted to meet his lawyer during interrogation though the latter may not be present throughout interrogation.

(11). A police control room should be provided at all district and State headquarters so that information regarding the arrest and the place of custody of the arrestee can be communicated by the officer carrying out the arrest within 12 hours of effecting the arrest and at the police control room it should be displayed on a conspicuous notice board.

**Pic. 3.2**

The Supreme Court also insists that the requirements that flow from of the Indian Constitution are to be strictly followed. These would apply with equal force to other Government agencies including the Directorate of Revenue Intelligence, Directorate of Enforcement, Coast Guard, Central Reserve Police Force (C.R.P.F), Border Security Force (B.S.F.) the Central Industrial Security Force (C.I.S.F), the State Armed Police, intelligence Agencies, such as the Intelligence Bureau, RAW, Central Bureau of Investigation (C.B.I.) and C.I.D. These guidelines are only a few out of a large number of judgments of the apex court in which the court upheld the human rights of the oppressed individuals.

**Pic. 3.3**

## Media and Human Rights

The information and media is an important arm of any modern democratic polity through which the people exercise their freedom of information. The freedom of information, the democratic right to know, is crucial in making all other human rights effective and providing an important safeguard for the enjoyment of all those rights. Traditionally, the vehicle of public information was the Press. Today, it is called the media, which include the press, the radio, the television and the internet. The 'Fourth Estate' plays a crucial role in a large democracy like India where about 1,500 different types of newspapers are circulated. The period of National Emergency saw, for the first time, the gagging of the free press. Many thing depended on the BBC for 'impartial' news about India. It is no wonder that the freedom of the press or media became a watchword after emergency. Disposing of a case of: contempt of court against the editors of two newspapers, the Supreme Court remarked, it is the duty of a true and responsible journalist to provide the people with accurate and impartial presentation of news and his views after dispassionate evacuation of facts and information received by him and to be published as a news item. The editor of a newspaper or a journal, the court said, has a greater responsibility to guard against untruthful news and its publication. If the newspaper publishes what is improper, mischievously false or illegal and abuses its liberty, it must be punished by a court of law. While a free and healthy press is indispensable to the functioning of a true democracy', however the court said, "The freedom of the press is subject to reasonable restraint." Since 1970s, the media in India have played a central role in sensitising people with information about governance, development, science and technology, foreign relations and so on. However, of late, it has also come in for criticism, as highlighted by the above Supreme Court decision. There has been decline in journalistic credibility, as noted by the Chairman of the Press Council of India himself in a seminar. Senior journalists feel that the media shies away from important 'people's issues like tribal issues, that it is losing social content and becoming a consumer product with a manager overshadowing the editor. While the media is "a vital leverage to keep the rulers in check," it has failed "to educate people to assert their claim to the right to information," observes another senior journalist. The press also has come in for rough treatment by terrorists, insurgents, and some individual politicians. The chairman of the Press Council condemned increasing commercialism and corrupt practices emphasising the need to arrest them. The media also has a tendency to launch 'trials by the media,' even sentencing by the media, even while a court proceeding is underway. Considering the totality of the impact of the media during the past two decades, despite the above pitfalls, one must recognise that the contribution of the media in revealing and highlighting human rights causes has been most impressive. A colonial law relating to official secrecy, The Official secrets act. 1923, however, remains an impediment in the effective exercise of the freedom of information.

# 4
# *Child Human Rights in India*

India is a party to the UN Declaration on the Rights of the Child, 1959. Accordingly, it adopted a National Policy on children in 1974. The policy reaffirmed the constitutional provisions for adequate services to children, both before and after birth and through the period of growth to ensure their full physical, mental and social development.

Accordingly, the government is taking actions to review the national and state legislation and bring it in line with the provisions of the Convention. It has also developed appropriate monitoring procedures to assess progress in implementing the Convention-involving various stakeholders in society.

India is also a signatory to the World Declaration on the Survival, Protection and Development of children. In pursuance of the commitment made at the World Summit, the Department of Women and Child Development under the Ministry of Human Resource Development has formulated a National Plan of Action for children. Most of the recommendations of the World Summit Action Plan are reflected in India's National Plan of Action keeping in mind the needs, rights and aspirations of 300 million children in the country. The priority areas in the Plan are health, nutrition, education, water, sanitation and environment. The Plan gives special consideration to children in difficult circumstances and aims at providing a framework for actualisation of the objectives of the Convention in the Indian context.

## Status of Children in India

A recent UNICEF (2005) report on the state of the world's children under the title 'Childhood Under Threat', speaking about India, states that millions of Indian children are equally deprived of their rights to survival, health, nutrition, education and safe drinking water. It is reported that 63 per cent of them go to bed hungry and 53 per cent suffer from chronic malnutrition.

The report says that 147 million children live in *kuchcha* houses, 77 million do not use drinking water from a tap, 85 million are not being immunised, 27 million are severely underweight and 33 million have never been to school. It estimates that 72 million children in India between five and 14 years do not have access to basic education. A girl child is the worst victim as she is often neglected and is discriminated against the preference for a boy child.

**Pic. 4.1**

## Child Rights

The Convention on the Rights of the Child defines basic rights of children covering multiple needs and issues. India endorsed it on December 11, 1992.

Following are a few rights in the immediate purview of Smile Foundation as well as India.

## Right to Education

Article 21A is a new human right, which is included in the Constitution by the eighty sixth Constitutions Amendment Act, 2002. In order to make the right to free and compulsory education to a child, the Constitution Amendment Bill 1997 was introduced in Rajya Sabha to insert a new Article 21A in the Constitution. However, the Bill was withdrawn on November 27th 2001. The Constitution 93rd amendment Bill, 2001 was introduced and passed by unanimous vote in the Lok Sabha on November 28th 2001 and in the Rajya Sabha on May 14th 2002 with formal amendments to 86th Constitutional amendment. According to Article 21A, the State shall provide free and compulsory education to all children of the age of six to fourteen years in such manner as the State may, by law, determine.

Before the constitutional process started for making the right to education a fundamental right, the Supreme Court in *J.P. Unni Krishnan and others v. The State of Andhra pradesh* held that every citizen of this country has the right to education until he completes the age of 14 years.

**Pic. 4.2**

***The Right to Education:*** 50 per cent of Indian children aged 6-14 do not go to school, dropout rates increase alarmingly in class III to V, with 50 per cent of boys and 58 per cent of girls.

**Pic. 4.3**

***The Right to Expression:*** Every child has a right to express himself freely in whichever way he likes. Majority of children, however, are exploited by their elders and not allowed to express.

***The Right to Information:*** Every child has a right to know his basic rights and his position in the society. High incidence of illiteracy and ignorance among the deprived and underprivileged children prevents them from having access to information about them and their society.

**Pic. 4.4**

***The Right to Nutrition:*** More than 50 per cent of India's children are malnourished. While one in every five adolescent boys is malnourished, one in every two girls in India is undernourished.

***The Right to Health and Care:*** 58 per cent of India's children below the age of two years are not fully vaccinated. And 24 per cent of these children do not receive any form of vaccination. Over 60 per cent of children in India are anaemic. 95 in every 1,000 children born in India do not see their fifth birthday. 70 in every 1,000 children born in India do not see their first birthday.

**Pic. 4.5**

***The Right to Protection from Abuse:*** There are approximately two million child commercial sex workers between the age of five and 15 years and about 3.3 million between 15 and 18 years. They form 40 per cent of the total population of commercial sex workers in India. 5,00,000 children are forced into this trade every year.

***The Right to Protection from Exploitation:*** 17 million children in India work as per official estimates. A study found that children were sent to work by compulsion and not by choice, mostly by parents, but with recruiters playing a crucial role in influencing decision. When working outside the family, children put in an average of 21 hours of labour per week. Poor and bonded families often 'sell' their children to contractors who promise lucrative jobs in the cities and the children end up being employed in brothels, hotels and domestic work. Many run away and find a life on the streets.

***The Right to Protection from Neglect:*** Every child has a right to lead a well-protected and secure life away from neglect. However, children working under exploitative and inhuman conditions get neglected badly.

***The Right to Development:*** Every child has a right to development that lets the child explore his/her full potential. Unfavorable living conditions of underprivileged children prevent them from growing in a free and uninhibited way.

***The Right to Recreation:*** Every child has a right to spend some time on recreational pursuits like sports, entertainment and hobbies to explore and develop. Majority of poor children in India do not get time to spend on recreational activities.

***The Right to Name and Nationality:*** Every child has a right to identify himself with a nation. A vast majority of underprivileged children in India are treated like commodities and exported to other countries as labourers or prostitutes.

***The Right to Survival:*** Of the 12 million girls born in India, three million do not see their fifteenth birthday, and a million of them are unable to survive even their first birthday. Every sixth girl child's death is due to gender discrimination.

## National Commission for Protection of Child Rights

In order to ensure child rights practices and in response to India's commitment to UN Declaration to this effect, the government of India set up a National Commission for Protection of Child Rights. The Commission is a statutory body notified under an Act of the Parliament on December 29, 2006. Besides the chairperson, it will have six members from the fields of child health, education, childcare and development, juvenile justice, children with disabilities, elimination of child labour, child psychology or sociology and laws relating to children. The Commission has the power to inquire into complaints and take *suo motu* notice of matters relating to deprivation of child's rights and non-implementation of laws providing for protection and development of children among other things. Aimed at examining and reviewing the safeguards provided by the law to protect child rights, the Commission will recommend measures for their effective implementation. It will suggest amendments, if needed, and look into complaints or take *suo motu* notice of cases of violation of the constitutional and legal rights of children.

The Commission is to ensure proper enforcement of child rights and effective implementation of laws and programmes relating to children enquiring into complaints and take *suo motu* cognizance of matters relating to deprivation of child rights; non-implementation of laws providing for protection and development of children and non-compliance of policy decisions, guidelines or instructions aimed at their welfare and announcing relief for children and issuing remedial measures to the state governments.

# 5
# *Human Rights of Women*

Human rights and fundamental freedoms are the birthright of all human beings; their protection and promotion is the first responsibility of governments.

**Pic. 5.1**

The World Conference on Human Rights reaffirmed the solemn commitment of all States to fulfill their obligation to promote universal respect observance and protection of all human rights and fundamental freedoms for all, in accordance with the Charter of the United Nations, other instruments relating to human rights, and international law. The universal nature of these rights and freedoms is beyond question.

The promotion and protection of all human rights and fundamental freedoms must be considered as a priority objective of the United Nations, in accordance with its purposes and principles, in particular with the purpose of international cooperation. In the framework of these purposes and principles, the promotion and protection of all human rights is a legitimate concern of the international community. The international community must treat human rights globally, in a fair and equal manner, on the same footing, and with the same emphasis. The platform for action reaffirms the importance of ensuring the universality, objectivity and non-selectivity of the consideration of human rights issues.

The platform for action reaffirms that all human rights—civil, cultural, economic, political and social, including the right to development—are universal, indivisible, and interdependent and interrelated, as expressed in the Vienna Declaration and Programme of Action adopted by the World Conference on Human Rights. The Conference reaffirmed that the human rights of women and the girl child are an inalienable, integral and indivisible part of universal human rights. The full and equal enjoyment of all human rights and fundamental freedoms by women and girls is a priority for Governments and the United Nations and is essential for the advancement of women.

Equal rights of men and women are explicitly mentioned in the preamble to the charter of the United Nations. All the major international human rights instruments include sex as one of the grounds upon which states may not discriminate.

## Violation Of Women Human Rights In India

Human rights are those minimum rights which are compulsorily obtainable by every individual as he/she is a member of human family. The Constitution of India also guarantees the equality of rights of men and women. However, in the sphere of women's human rights in India, there exists a wide gulf between theory and practice. Indian society is a male dominated society where men are always assumed to be superior in society. The women in India very often have to face discrimination, injustice and dishonour. Though, women in India have been given more rights as compared to men, even then the condition of women in India is miserable. The study will throw light on the human rights of women in India and that how all the fundamental rights given

Pic. 5.2

to the women are being violated in India, by focussing on the various crimes done against them.

The Constitution of India has granted equal rights to the men and women. According to article 14, the State shall not deny to any person equality before law or the equal protection of laws within the territory of India. And Article 15 states, State shall not discriminate against any citizen on grounds only of religion, race, caste, sex, place of birth or any of them. But today, it seems that there is a wide gulf between theory and practice. The women in India have always been considered subordinate to men. Though, the articles contained in the Constitution mandates equality and non—discrimination on the grounds of sex, women is always discriminated and dishonoured in Indian society. Although, various efforts have been taken to improve the status of women in India, the constitutional dream of gender equality is still miles away from becoming a reality.

Though, human rights are the minimum rights which are compulsorily obtainable by every individual as he/she is a member of human society. But it has been found that each and every right of the women is being violated in one or another way. The crimes against women in India are increasing at a very fast pace. The National Crime Records Bureau (NCRB) had predicted that growth rate of crime against women would be higher than the population growth by 2010, which was found to be true. The Table below represents a list of top five most dangerous cities in India in terms of crimes against women.

**Table 5.1** **Five Most Dangerous cities in India in terms of crimes against Women**

| *RANK* | *NAME OF THE CITY* | *PERCENTAGE OF CRIMES AGAINST WOMEN IN INDIAN CITIES* |
|---|---|---|
| 1st | DELHI | 16 |
| 2nd | HYDRABAD | 8.1 |
| 3rd | BANGALORE | 6.5 |
| 4th | AHMADABAD | 6.4 |
| 5th | MUMBAI | 5.8 |

There is a need to discuss the rights of the women separately as women represent more than half the population of India, yet they are discriminated in every sphere of her life. Only women are a prey to crimes such as rape, dowry, death, sexual harassment, selling and importation, prostitution and trafficking, etc. Have you heard the men as a victim to all these crimes? The answer is a big 'No'. This year there has been 20 per cent increase in women trafficking, procurement of minor girls accounted for 19.8 per cent, importation of girls accounted for 4.9 per cent, and buying of girls for prostitution accounted for 2.3 per cent approx. Then how these human rights are beneficial to women? Though, government is taking a number of steps to improve the condition of women in India, but there is still a long way to go.

**Pic. 5.3**

The study revaluated the various human rights of women in India and how they are being violated. Although special rights are being given to woman as compared to men, yet they are least beneficial to them.

**WOMEN HUMAN RIGHTS IN INDIA**

- Right to equality.
- Right to education.
- Right to live with dignity.
- Right to liberty.
- Right to politics.
- Right to property.
- Right to equal opportunity for employment.
- Right to free choice of profession.
- Right to livelihood.
- Right to work in equitable condition.

- Right to get equal wages for equal work.
- Right to protection from gender discrimination.
- Right to social protection in the eventuality of retirement, old age and sickness.
- Right to protection from inhuman treatment.
- Right to protection of health.
- Right to privacy in terms of personal life, family, residence, correspondence, etc. and.
- Right to protection from society, state and family system.

**Violation of Women Human Rights**

It has been repeatedly said these days that women in India are enjoying the rights equal to men. But in reality, the women in India have been the sufferers from past. Not only in earlier times but even now a days have women to face discrimination, injustice and dishonour. Let us now discuss the crimes done against women in spite of being given rights equal to men. These points will explain that it in broad daylight continues violation of human rights against women in India.

**Pic. 5.4**

**Violation of Women Human Rights in Past**

The exploitation of women in India is not the present phenomenon. Rather 'she' is being exploited from the earlier times. The women in Indian society never stood for a fair status. The following crimes were done against the women in the past times.

## Devadasi

*Devadasi* was a religious practice in some parts of southern India, in which women were married to a deity of temples. In the later period, the illegitimate sexual exploitation of the *devadasi* became a norm in some part of the country.

**Pic. 5.5**

Jauhar

*Jauhar* refers to practice of the voluntary immolation of all wives and daughters of defeated warriors in order to avoid capture and consequent molestation by the enemy. The practice was followed by the wives of Rajput rulers, who are known to place a high premium on honour.

Purdah

*Purdah* is a practice among some communities requiring women to cover their bodies so as to cover their skin and conceal their form. It curtails their right to interact freely and it is a symbol of the subordination of women.

Sati

*Sati* is an old custom in Indian society in which widows were immolated alive on her husband's funeral pyre. Although the act

**Pic. 5.6**

was supposed to be voluntary on the widow's part, it is believed to have been sometimes forced on the widow.

Governments must not only refrain from violating the human rights of all women, but must work actively to promote and protect these rights. Recognition of the importance of the human rights of women is reflected in the fact that three quarters of the state members of the United Nations have become parties to the Convention on the elimination of all forms of discrimination against women.

The World Conference on Human Rights reaffirmed clearly that the human rights of women throughout the life cycle are an inalienable, integral and indivisible part of universal human rights. The International Conference on population and development reaffirmed women's reproductive rights and the right to development. Both the Declaration of the rights of the child and the Convention on the rights of the child guarantee children's rights and uphold the principle of non-discrimination on the grounds of gender.

The gap between the existence of rights and their effective enjoyment derives from a lack of commitment by governments to promoting and protecting those rights and the failure to inform women and men alike about them. The lack of appropriate recourse mechanisms at the national and international levels, and inadequate resources at both levels compound the problem. In most countries, steps have been taken to reflect the rights guaranteed by the Convention on the elimination of all forms of discrimination

**Pic. 5.7**

against women in national law. A number of countries have established mechanisms to strengthen women's ability to exercise their rights.

In order to protect the human rights of women, it is necessary to avoid, as far as possible, resorting to reservations and to ensure that no reservation is incompatible with the object and purpose of the Convention or is otherwise incompatible with international treaty law. Unless the human rights of women, as defined by international human rights instruments, are fully recognised and effectively protected, applied, implemented and enforced in national law as well as in national practice in family, civil, penal, labour and commercial codes and administrative rules and regulations, they will exist in name only.

In those countries that have not yet become parties to the Convention on the elimination of all forms of discrimination against women and other international human rights instruments, or where reservations that are incompatible with the object or purpose of the convention have been entered, or where national laws have not yet been revised to implement international norms and standards, women's de jure equality is not yet secured. Women's full enjoyment of equal rights is undermined by the discrepancies between some national legislation and international law and international instruments on human rights. Overly complex administrative procedures, lack of awareness within the judicial process and inadequate monitoring of the violation of the human rights of all women, coupled with the under-representation of women in justice systems, insufficient information on existing rights and persistent attitudes and practices perpetuate women's *de facto* inequality. *De facto* inequality is also perpetuated by the lack of enforcement of *inter alia* family, civil, penal, labour and commercial laws or codes, or administrative rules and regulations intended to ensure women's full enjoyment of human rights and fundamental freedoms.

Every person should be entitled to participate in, contribute to and enjoy cultural, economic, political and social development. In many cases women and girls suffer discrimination in the allocation of economic and social resources. This directly violates their economic, social and cultural rights.

The human rights of all women and the girl child must form an integral part of United Nations human rights activities. Intensified efforts are needed to integrate the equal status and the human rights of all women and girls into the mainstream of United Nations system-wide activities and to address these issues regularly and systematically throughout relevant bodies and mechanisms. This requires *inter alia* improved cooperation and coordination between the commissions on the status of women, and other provisions like the United Nations high commissioner for Human Rights, the commission on Human Rights, including its special and thematic rapporteurs, independent experts, working groups and its sub commission on prevention of discrimination and protection of minorities, the commission on sustainable development, the commission for social development, the commission on crime prevention and criminal justice, and the committee on the elimination of discrimination against women and other human rights treaty bodies, and all relevant entities of the United Nations system, including the specialised agencies. Cooperation is also needed to strengthen, rationalise and streamline the United Nations human rights system and to promote its effectiveness and efficiency, taking into account the need to avoid unnecessary duplication and overlapping of mandates and tasks.

If the goal of full realisation of human rights for all is to be achieved, international human rights instruments must be applied in such a way as to take more clearly into consideration the systematic and systemic nature of discrimination against women that gender analysis has clearly indicated.

**Pic. 5.8**

Bearing in mind the programme of action of the International Conference on population and development and the Vienna Declaration and programme of action adopted by the World Conference on Human Rights, the fourth World Conference on women reaffirms that reproductive rights rest on the recognition of the basic right of all couples and individuals to decide freely and responsibly the number, spacing and timing of their children and to have the information and means to do so, and the right to attain the highest standard of sexual and reproductive health. It also includes their right to make decisions concerning reproduction free of discrimination, coercion and violence, as expressed in human rights documents.

Violence against women both violates and impairs or nullifies the enjoyment by women of human rights and fundamental freedoms. Taking into account the declaration on the elimination of violence against women and the work of special rapporteurs, gender-based violence, such as battering and other domestic violence, sexual abuse, sexual slavery and exploitation, and international trafficking in women and children, forced prostitution and sexual harassment, as well as violence against women, resulting from cultural prejudice, racism and racial discrimination, xenophobia, pornography, ethnic cleansing, armed conflict, foreign occupation, religious and anti-religious extremism and terrorism are incompatible with the dignity and the worth of the human existence and must be combated and eliminated. Any harmful aspect of certain traditional, customary or modern practices that violates the rights of women should be prohibited and eliminated. Governments should take urgent action to combat and eliminate all forms of violence against women in private and public life, whether perpetrated or tolerated by the state or private persons.

Many women face additional barriers to the enjoyment of their human rights because of factors such as race, language, ethnicity, culture, religion, disability or socio-economic class, or because they are indigenous people, migrants including women workers, displaced women or refugees. They may also be disadvantaged and marginalised by a general lack of knowledge and recognition of their human rights as well as by the obstacles they meet in gaining access to information and recourse mechanisms in cases of violation of their rights.

The factors that cause the flight of refugee women, other displaced women in need of international protection and internally displaced women may be different from those affecting men. These women continue to be vulnerable to abuses of their human rights during and after their flight.

While women are increasingly using the legal system to exercise their rights, in many countries lack of awareness of the existence of these rights is an obstacle that prevents women from fully enjoying their human rights and attaining equality. Experience in many countries has shown that women can be empowered and motivated to assert their rights, regardless of their level of education or socio-economic status. Legal literacy programmes and media strategies have been effective in helping women to understand the link between their rights and other aspects of their lives, and in demonstrating that cost-effective initiatives can be undertaken to help women obtain those rights. Provision of human rights education is essential for promoting an understanding of the human rights of women, including knowledge of recourse mechanisms to redress violations of their rights. It is necessary for all individuals, especially women in vulnerable circumstances, to have full knowledge of their rights and access to legal recourse against violations of their rights.

Women engaged in the defence of human rights must be protected. Governments have a duty to guarantee the full enjoyment of all rights set out in the Universal Declaration of human rights, the International Covenant on civil and political rights, and the International Covenant on economic, social and cultural rights by women working peacefully in a personal or organisational capacity for the promotion and protection of human rights. Non-governmental organisations, women's organisations and feminist groups have played a catalyc role in the promotion of the human rights of women through grass-roots activities, networking and advocacy and need encouragement, support and access to information from governments in order to carry out these activities.

In addressing the enjoyment of human rights, governments and other actors should promote an active and visible policy of mainstreaming a gender perspective in all policies and programmes so that, before decisions are taken, an analysis is made of the effects, on women and men, respectively. Work actively towards ratification of or accession to and implement international and regional human rights treaties; ratify and accede to and ensure implementation of the Convention on the elimination of all forms of discrimination against women so that universal ratification of the Convention can be achieved by the year 2000; limit the extent of any reservations to the Convention on the elimination of all forms of discrimination against women; formulate any such reservations as precisely and as narrowly as possible; ensure that no reservations are incompatible with the object and purpose of the Convention or otherwise incompatible with international treaty law and regularly review them with a view to withdrawing them; and withdraw reservations that are contrary to the object and purpose of the Convention on the elimination of all forms of discrimination against women, or which are otherwise incompatible with international treaty law; consider drawing up national action plans identifying steps to improve the promotion and protection of human rights, including the human rights of women, as recommended by the World Conference on human rights; create or strengthen independent national institutions for the protection and promotion of these rights, including the human rights of women, as recommended by the World Conference on human rights; develop a comprehensive human rights education programme to raise awareness among women of their human rights and raise awareness among others of the human rights of women; if they are states parties, implement the Convention by reviewing all national laws, policies, practices and procedures to ensure that they meet the obligations set out in the Convention; all states should undertake a review of all national laws, policies, practices and procedures to ensure that they meet international human rights obligations in this matter; include gender aspects in reporting under all other human rights conventions and instruments, including ILO conventions, to ensure analysis and review of the human rights of women; report on schedule to the committee on the elimination of discrimination against women regarding the implementation of the Convention, following fully the guidelines established by the committee and involving non-governmental organisations, where appropriate, or taking into account their contributions in the preparation of the report; enable the committee on the elimination of discrimination against women fully to discharge its mandate by allowing for adequate meeting time through broad ratification of the revision adopted by the state parties to the Convention on the elimination of all forms of discrimination against women on 22nd May, 1995 relative to Article 20(1), and by promoting efficient working methods; support the process initiated by the commission on the status of women with a view to elaborately a draft an optional protocol to the Convention on the elimination of all forms of discrimination against women that could enter into force as soon as possible on a right of petition-procedure, taking into consideration the Secretary- general's report on the optional protocol, including those views related to its feasibility; address the acute problems of children *inter alia* by supporting efforts in the context of the United Nations system aimed at adopting efficient international measures for the prevention and eradication of female infanticide, harmful child labour, the sale of children and their organs, child prostitution, child pornography and other forms of sexual abuse, and consider contributing to the drafting of an optional protocol to the Convention on the rights of the child; strengthen the implementation of all relevant human rights instruments in order to combat and eliminate, including through international cooperation, organised and other forms of trafficking in women and children, including trafficking for the purposes of sexual exploitation, pornography, prostitution and sex tourism, and provide legal and social services to the victims; this should include provisions for international cooperation to prosecute and punish those responsible for organised exploitation of women and children; taking into account the need to ensure full respect for the human rights of indigenous women; consider a declaration on the rights of indigenous people for adoption by the general assembly within the International decade of the world's indigenous people; and encourage the participation of indigenous women in the working group elaborating the draft declaration, in accordance with the provisions for the participation of organisations of indigenous people.

By relevant organs, bodies and agencies of the United Nations system, all human rights bodies of the United Nations system, as well as the United Nations High Commissioner for Human Rights and the United Nations High Commissioner for Refugees, while promoting greater efficiency and effectiveness through better coordination of the various bodies, mechanisms and procedures, taking into account the need to avoid unnecessary duplication and overlapping of their mandates and tasks: give full, equal and sustained attention to the human rights of women in the exercise of their respective mandates to promote universal respect for and protection of all human rights; civil, cultural, economic, political and social rights, including the right to development; ensure the implementation of the recommendations of the World Conference on Human Rights for the full integration and mainstreaming of the human rights of women; develop a comprehensive policy programme for mainstreaming the human rights of women throughout the United Nations system, including activities with regard to advisory services, technical assistance, reporting methodology, gender-impact assessments, coordination, public information and human rights education, and play an active role in the implementation of the programme; ensure the integration and full participation of women as both agents and beneficiaries in the development process and reiterate the objectives established for global action for women towards sustainable and equitable development set forth in the Rio Declaration on environment and development. Include information on gender-based human rights violations in their activities and integrate the findings into all of their programmes and activities; ensure that there is collaboration and coordination of the work of all human rights bodies and mechanisms to ensure that the human rights of women are respected; strengthen cooperation and coordination between the Commission on the status of women, the Commission on human rights, the Commission for social development, the Commission on sustainable development, the Commission on crime prevention and criminal justice, the United Nations human rights treaty monitoring bodies, including the Committee on the elimination of discrimination against women, and the United Nations development fund for women, the International Research and Training Institute for the Advancement of Women, the United Nations Development Programme, the United Nations Children's Fund and other organisations of the United Nations system, acting within their mandates, in the promotion of the human rights of women, and improve cooperation between the Division for the Advancement of Women and the Centre for Human Rights; establish effective cooperation between the United Nations High Commissioner for Human Rights and the United Nations High Commissioner for Refugees and other relevant bodies, within their respective mandates, taking into account the close link between massive violations of human rights, especially in the form of genocide, ethnic cleansing, systematic rape of women in war situations and refugee flows and other displacements, and the fact that refugee, displaced and returnee women may be subject to particular human rights abuse; encourage incorporation of a gender perspective in national programmes of action and in human rights and national institutions, within the context of human rights advisory services programmes; provide training in the human rights of women for all United Nations personnel and officials, especially those in human rights and humanitarian relief activities, and promote their understanding of the human rights of women so that they recognise and deal with violations of the human rights of women and can fully take into account the gender aspect of their work; in reviewing the implementation of the plan of action for the United Nations Decade for Human Rights Education (1995-2004), take into account the results of the Fourth World Conference on Women.

**By Governments**

(a). Give priority to promoting and protecting the full and equal enjoyment by women and men of all human rights and fundamental freedoms without distinction of any kind as to race, colour, sex, language, religion, political or other opinions, national or social origins, property, birth or other status;

(b). Provide constitutional guarantees and/or enact appropriate legislation to prohibit discrimination on the basis of sex for all women and girls of all ages and assure women of all ages equal rights and their full enjoyment;

(c). Embody the principle of the equality of men and women in their legislation and ensure, through law and other appropriate means, the practical realisation of this principle;

(d). Review national laws, including customary laws and legal practices in the areas of family, civil, penal, labour and commercial law in order to ensure the implementation of the principles and procedures of all relevant international human rights instruments by means of national legislation, revoke any remaining laws that discriminate on the basis of sex and remove gender bias in the administration of justice;

(e). Strengthen and encourage the development of programmes to protect the human rights of women in the national institutions on human rights that carry out programmes, such as human rights commissions or ombudspersons, according to the appropriate status, resources and access to the government to assist individuals, in particular women, and ensure that these institutions pay adequate attention to problems involving the violation of the human rights of women;

(f). Take action to ensure that the human rights of women, are fully respected and protected;

(g). Take urgent action to combat and eliminate violence against women, which is a human rights violation, resulting from harmful traditional or customary practices, cultural prejudices and extremism;

(h). Prohibit female genital mutilation wherever it exists and give vigourous support to efforts among non-governmental and community organisations and religious institutions to eliminate such practices;

(i). Provide gender-sensitive human rights education and training to public officials, including *inter alia* police and military personnel, correction officers, health and medical personnel, and social workers, including people who deal with migration and refugee issues, and teachers at all levels of the educational system, and make available such education and training also to the judiciary and members of parliament in order to enable them to better exercise their public responsibilities;

(j). Promote the equal right of women to be members of trade unions and other professional and social organisations;

(k). Establish effective mechanisms for investigating violations of the human rights of women perpetrated by any public official and take the necessary punitive legal measures in accordance with national laws;

(l). Review and amend criminal laws and procedures, as necessary, to eliminate any discrimination against women in order to ensure that criminal law and procedures guarantee women effective protection against, and prosecution of, crimes directed at or disproportionately affecting women, regardless of the relationship between the perpetrator and the victim, and ensure that women defendants, victims and/or witnesses are not revictimised or discriminated against in the investigation and prosecution of crimes;

(m). Ensure that women have the same right as men to be judges, advocates or other officers of the court, as well as police officers and prison and detention officers, among other things;

(n). Strengthen existing or establish readily available and free or affordable alternative administrative mechanisms and legal aid programmes to assist disadvantaged women seeking redress for violations of their rights;

(o). Ensure that all women and non-governmental organisations and their members in the field of protection and promotion of all human rights—civil, cultural, economic, political and social rights, including the right to development; enjoy fully all human rights and freedoms in accordance with the Universal Declaration of Human Rights and all other human rights instruments and the protection of national laws;

(p). Strengthen and encourage the implementation of the recommendations contained in the Standard Rules on the Equalisation of Opportunities for Persons with Disabilities, paying special attention to ensure non-discrimination and equal enjoyment of all human rights and fundamental freedoms by women and girls with disabilities, including their access to information and services in the field of violence against women, as well as their active participation in and economic contribution to all aspects of society;

(q). Encourage the development of gender-sensitive human rights programmes.

**By Governments and Non-governmental Organisations, the United Nations and other International Organisations, as Appropriate**

(a). Translate, whenever possible, into local and indigenous languages and into alternative formats appropriate for persons with disabilities and persons at lower levels of literacy; publicise and disseminate laws and information relating to the equal status and human rights of all women, including the Universal Declaration of Human Rights, the International Covenant on Civil and Political Rights, the International Covenant on Economic, Social and Cultural Rights, the Convention on the Elimination of all forms of Discrimination against Women, the International Convention on the Elimination of all forms of Racial Discrimination, the Convention on the Rights of the Child, the Convention against Torture and Other Cruel, Inhuman or Degrading Treatment or Punishment, the Declaration on the Right to Development and the Declaration on the Elimination of Violence against Women, as well as the outcomes of relevant United Nations conferences and summits and national reports to the Committee on the Elimination of Discrimination against Women;

(b). Publicise and disseminate such information in easy understandable formats and alternative formats appropriate for persons with disabilities, and persons at low levels of literacy;

(c). Disseminate information on national legislation and its impact on women, including easily accessible guidelines on how to use a justice system to exercise one's rights;

(d). Include information about international and regional instruments and standards in their public information and human rights education activities and in adult education and training programmes, particularly for groups such as the military, the police and other law enforcement personnel, the judiciary, and legal and health professionals to ensure that human rights are effectively protected;

(e). Make widely available and fully publicised information on the existence of national, regional and international mechanisms for seeking redress when the human rights of women are violated;

(f). Encourage, coordinate and cooperate with local and regional women's groups, relevant non-governmental organisations, educators and the media, to implement programmes in human rights education to make women aware of their human rights;

(g). Promote education on the human and legal rights of women in school curricula at all levels of education and undertake public campaigns, including in the most widely used languages of the country, on the equality of women and men in public and private life, including their rights within the family and relevant human rights instruments under national and international law;

(h). Promote education in all countries in human rights and international humanitarian law for members of the national security and armed forces, including those assigned to United Nations peace-keeping operations, on a routine and continuing basis, reminding them and sensitising them to the fact that they should respect the rights of women at all times, both on and off duty, giving special attention to the rules on the protection of women and children and to the protection of human rights in situations of armed conflict;

(i). Take appropriate measures to ensure that refugee and displaced women, migrant women and migrant women workers are made aware of their human rights and of the recourse mechanisms available to them.

(j). The National Commission for Women (NCW) is a statutory body for women established in 1992 by Government of India under the provisions of the Indian Constitution, as defined in the 1990, National Commission for Women Act. The first head of the Commission was Ms Jayanti Patnaik. The objective of the NCW is to represent the rights of women in India and to provide a voice for their issues and concerns. The subjects of their campaigns have included dowry, politics, religion, equal representation for women in jobs, and the exploitation of women for labour. They have also discussed police abuses against women.

The commission regularly publishes a monthly newsletter, *Rashtra Mahila* in both Hindi and English.

# 6
# Sexual Assault in India

In India, rape, sexual harassment, and the abuse of women are common occurrences that go unspoken. Despite escalating public outcry against rape, reported cases have increased steadily, with the only slight decline occurring in 2009. In 2013, reports of rape increased 35 per cent from the previous year. The meaning of the data is difficult to judge, as increased awareness may mean less stigma in reporting rape cases. Figures are based on reported crimes documented by the National Crime Record Bureau of India updated on July 1st, 2014.

**Pic. 6.1**

*Sources:* National Crime Records Bureau: Crime in India, 2013: Crimes Against Women.

National Crime Records Bureau: Figures at a Glance, 2012.
National Crime Records Bureau, 2011 Stats (PDF).
National Crime Records Bureau, 2010 Stats (PDF).
National Crime Records Bureau, 2009 Stats (PDF).
National Crime Records Bureau, 2008 Stats (PDF).
National Crime Records Bureau, 2007 Stats (PDF).
NIPCCD: Statistics on Women in India, 2010.
Gulbarga University: Violence Against Women in India (PDF).

*Sources:* National Crime Records Bureau: Table-12.12. Disposal of Persons Arrested Under IPC Crimes By Courts During 2013.

**Graphics. 6.1**

27 percent is the conviction rate for rape accused in India (2013). Rape is often notoriously difficult to prove in court, with the victim forced to endure a 'second rape' by a zealous legal defence aimed at discrediting her. In 2013, every third of rape cases brought to court in India resulted in a conviction. Updated: July 1st, 2014.

70 per cent of women living in India endure some form of domestic abuse. According to a report by the Mumbai-based rights organisation Dasra, over half of Indian women have suffered some form of domestic abuse at the hands of a husband or relative. Domestic violence accounts for 50 per cent of total reported crimes against women in the country. Additionally, in 2014, an Indian high court ruled that marital rape is not a crime. Updated: July 1st, 2014.

*Sources:* Dasra: No Private Matter: Confronting Domestic Violence in India. Kidnapping and Bodily Harm Against Women (2007-2013).

India is one of the most dangerous places in the world for women to live, as evidenced by the shocking rates of various types of abuse, including hitting, kicking, choking, hair pulling, and burning. Dowry deaths, when a wife dies from burns, bodily harm, or any other unnatural circumstance at the hand of her husband or other relatives, also occur. Updated: July 1st, 2014.

*Sources:*

IPS News: Violence Against Women Surging in India.
National Crime Records Bureau: 2011 Stats (PDF).
National Crime Records Bureau: 2010 Stats (PDF).
National Crime Records Bureau: 2009 Stats (PDF).
National Crime Records Bureau: 2008 Stats (PDF).
National Crime Records Bureau: 2007 Stats (PDF).
NIPCCD: Statistics on Women in India 2010.
Gulbarga University: Violence Against Women in India (PDF).

20 years is the new maximum prison sentence for rape. Mass anti-rape protests broke out and have continued in response to the December 2012 gang-rape of a 23 year-old woman in Delhi, who eventually died from the injuries she sustained during the assault. Security forces have cracked down on protests by using water cannons, tear gas, and long sticks to disperse crowds. In early February 2013, the Indian government passed a new sexual violence law that increased the maximum sentence for rape to 20 years, and in cases where the victim dies or goes into a coma, the death penalty. This has led to further protests as activists point out the new law does not address a multitude of issues, including marital rape.

**Graphics. 6.2**

*Sources: Sky News:* Activists protest against Indian rape law. Every day, 93 women are raped in India according to the latest figures presented by the NCRB, 93 rapes are reported every single day in India. Updated: July 1st, 2014 from National Crime Records Bureau: Crime in India, 2013: Crimes Against Women.

**Graphics. 6.3**

States and Territories with the Highest Incidence of Reported Rape (2013):

- Madhya Pradesh 4,335 reported rapes.
- Rajasthan 3,285 reported rapes.
- Maharashtra 3,063 reported rapes.
- Uttar Pradesh 3,050 and Assam 1,937 reported rape.

According to statistics published by the National Crime Records Bureau, India in 2014. Updated: July 1st, 2014.

*Sources:* National Crime Records Bureau: Table-5.1 Incidence and Rate of Crime Committed Against Women in States, UTs and Cities during 2013.

Rapists by Relationship to Victim (2013):

- Parents or close family members two per cent

- Relatives seven per cent
- Neighbours 34 per cent
- Other known persons 57 per cent

These figures are only representative of cases in which the victim knows the attacker, and do not account for the 6 percent of incidences in which the assailant is unknown. Updated: July 1, 2014.

*Sources:* National Crime Records Bureau: Offenders Relation and Proximity to Rape Victims, 2013.

94 per cent of rape victims know their attacker of the 33,707 rapes reported in India in 2013, a staggering 31,807 cases involved somebody the victim knew. Updated: July 1st, 2014.

**Graphics. 6.4**

*Sources:* NCRB: Figures at a Glance - 2012.

NCRB: Offenders Relation and proximity to Rape Victims, 2012.

# 7

# Types of Human Rights

The human rights are not uniform and equal to each citizen of India. The following observations during field visits suggest that the human rights prevalent in India are of the following category:

(1). Differential Human Rights; are such human rights which creates difference among human rights.
(2). Discriminatory Human Rights; are such human rights which discriminates among citizen instead of uniformity.
(3). Deprivatory Human Rights; are such human rights which deprive human beings in course of getting human rights.

In the following pages the field experiences has been given which will substantiate the above classification.

## Case observation-1

The Central Jail, Raipur is one of the oldest jail in the country set up during the British period in the year 1882 by the British Government, and Dr Bhesle, the then Civil Surgeon, Raipur was appointed as the first superintendent of the jail. It became functional in 1885 but the district Gazetteer mentions that the construction of the jail building started in 1862 and was completed in 1868. In 1923, Raipur jail was given the status of district jail and in 1956, it was made central jail.

There are 30 jails in the state in which five are central jails, 10 are district jails and 15 are sub-jails in which 28 are functional and two sub-jails i.e., Sukma and Narayanpur are temporarily closed.

The capacity of the jails in the state is of 6,040 (5,559 Male and 481 Female), but as on 31.08.2013, total number of prisoners were 15,396 (14,682 male and 714 female. 9,542 prisoners were more than the capacity of the jails. This deserves NHRC attention.

***Under-trial Prisoners:*** There are 8,830 under-trail prisoners in the jails of Chhattisgarh which is 57.35 per cent of the total prisoners.

***Mentally Ill Prisoners:*** There are one case each in Raipur and Bilaspur central jail suffering from schizophrenic disease and 152 are mentally sick which requires treatment by clinical psychologists.

There is no clinical psychologists or MBBS doctors specially trained for treating psychological cases in the jails of Chhattisgarh. Therefore it is felt that such doctors may be appointed in each jail of Chhattisgarh.

***Foreign National Prisoners:*** There is only one foreign national prisoner in the Bilaspur jail. His speedy trial may help the prisoners in getting justice in time.

***Prisoners of Other States:*** There are 458 prisoners of other states in the jails of Chhattisgarh.

***Acquitted Mentally Ill Prisoners:*** There are two acquitted mentally ill prisoners in Chhattisgarh, one from central jail, Raipur and another from central jail, Jagdalpur.

***Video Conference Facility:*** The video conference facility is available in 13 jails of Chhattisgarh.

***Water Supply and Sanitation:*** It has been observed during visit of Raipur central jail and Bilaspur jail that the prisoners as well as under-trail prisoners are using old pitchers, tin or plastic containers to store water in their wards for drinking purpose. When requested to show such containers it was found that those were contaminated leading to water-borne disease. This deserves attention of concerned agency.

***Cleanliness in Jail:*** It has been observed during visit that the toilets and bathrooms of the prisoners need to be cleaned properly, the manpower be also increased as per the number of inmates of jail and vacant post be filled immediately.

The prisoners are given soap and oil for their physical cleanliness. Women prisoners be also given hair removers.

***Food Supply:***

***Board of Visitors:***

***Women Prisoners:*** There are 714 women prisoners in which 283 are convicted and 431 are under-trial. Women prisoners are lodged in women wards. Only women officers and staff are posted in the women wards. Male officers can visit only in the presence of women officers.

***Women Provisos with Child:*** 74 children are living with women prisoners.

***Death in Jail:*** Three prisoners died. All were natural death.

***Present Security:*** It has been reported that naxalites are training fellow prisoners and break of jail is likely; it deserves attention of concerned authority.

***Parole:*** 446 prisoners were granted parole in 2013.

***New Facilities:*** Jail hospital, doctor on service, vacant post. 18 posts of doctor are vacant.

***Education in jail:***

### *Observations and Recommendations*

(1). It has been observed that the overcrowding is a common sight. The prisoners are living as animal on many occasions; it has been found that the prisoners do not have adequate space to sleep in the wards. The total numbers of prisoners in the jails of Chhattisgarh are three times more than the capacity of the jails.

(2). The post of doctors are vacant, it needs to be filled up immediately. Number of women doctors should be increased in proportion to women prisoners.

(3). There are no skin specialist and clinical psychologist; specialist medical officers and paramedical personnel be appointed immediately as the incidence of skin disease and mental cases are increasing day by day.

(4). It has been observed that old and dirty earthen pitchers, containers of tin, plastic jars or buckets or bottles were found in the prisoners wards filled with water which they use for drinking purpose. This need immediate attention.

(5). The Naxal prisoners deserve special attention of jail authority as they are giving training to fellow prisoners and are preparing for, as reported, jail-break.

(6). There are 316 sanctioned posts in central jail, Raipur, against 152 posts are vacant. This may be filled immediately. Similarly, in Bilaspur jail sanctioned posts are 202 in which 117 posts are vacant; it should be filled up without any delay.

(7). The vocational training imparted to prisoners is good and needs to be followed by other jails.

(8). Jail ought to be designed for the development of the human quality and virtues among prisoners.

(9). Fast-track court needs to be established to minimise the number of under-trial prisoners.

(10). Cases of young boys and girls pursuing their study of medical, management, engineering, etc. be taken up by the fast-track court and to support them in completing their studies.

(11). A careful consideration is required for dowry cases.

## University

Vice chancellors of universities, head of departments of almost all faculties and disciplines, registrar of universities, director of higher education of govts and a good number of students with whom i interacted, it emerged commonly that.

The concept of human rights in educational institutions was not very clear to the faculty members of the university. Even the head of the law faculty had limited clarity of the human rights in changing scenario.

However, the students of the university raised several questions relating to the human rights in getting admission as some students from general caste category were admitted on the reserved seats of SC/ST as the adequate number from these categories did not turn up at time for admission, but came after last date of admission.

Similarly, their questions were related to ragging, teasing of girl students, non-availability of books in the library, examination system, etc. The university staff raised questions on their promotions, transfers, appointment, etc.

On the whole, the vice-chancellor said that it was a good educative-interactive session for them; further requested for organising awareness camp on the campus while admission time so that in the very beginning students can be made aware of their human rights which may minimise many problems of the university.

### *Recommendation*

An awareness camp of human rights in the university may be organised in different universities to make younger generation well aware of the respective.

# Case Observation-2

Went to the village, remotely located, met the villagers and also Mr Gupta and then came to *Panchyat Bhawan* of the village where more than 500 villagers both male and female were waiting. All sub-divisional officers, block officers and officers at the *panchyat* and village level were also present.

## Observations

(1). Mr Vinod Kr Gupta 48 year old is M.Sc. LL.B. and owns 2.50 acres of land in his name and have share in paternal agricultural land also which is in the name of his mother.

(2). Mr. Jagdesh Tiwari is the manager of *sewa sahkari samiti.*

(3). In group interview it emerged that the villagers are divided mainly in two groups.

One grouped by Mr Vinod Kr Gupta.
Second led by Sri Jagdesh Tiwari and both groups. act against each other and criticise each other just to show supremacy ever each other.

(4). Mr Gupta said that the agriculture of village is badly affected by drought for last three years; animals from close forest (village is situated in forest area) destroy their agriculture; seeds, pesticides and fertilisers are not supplied in time. Most of the villagers complained the same.

(5). Training of modern agriculture practices is not given to the farmers of the village. It was said in the presence of all those officers and media persons.

(6). The FIR of the villagers is not recorded by the local police station.

(7). It appears that there is personal animosity between Mr Vinod Kumar Gupta and Sri Jagdeesh Tiwari.

(8). Three years back Mr Gupta filed papers for getting elected as office bearer of the co-operative society of Chilhari but he could not because he is not, the member of the co-operative, this further fuelled the animosity between Mr Vinod Gupta and Sri Jagdeesh Tiwari.

(9). The public distribution system of the village generally is not distributing kerosene oil, wheat, rice, suger and salt properly, and the quality of the commodities are of inferior quality, difficult for human to eat.

(10). Mr Vinod Kumar Gupta is not having KCC card because he never applied for it. When I requested him that please give an application to the sub divisional officer, who was present in *panchyat Bhawan* so that he may get a KCC card but he refused.

(11). Mr Vinod Kumar Gupta and also other villagers have no idea what human rights mean for.

(12). It has been observed that corruption at the village and *panchayat* level institutions are rampant because of the corrupt system. The public distribution outlets distribute when they get from block level officers similarly, block level officers distribute when they get from district level officers, and district level officers distribute when they get from state level officers. They distribute grains, kerosene oil, salt. If it is delayed from state level then it is also delayed at village level. This delay leads to corruption. Seeds are required when rain is there but it is not necessary that at that time Government. institutions/Cooperative society will have seeds, fertilisers, pesticides to distribute, even if they have and they distribute the quality inferior which puts farmers to loss. Government need to change the system.

(13). Corruption in cooperative society is rampant because the person is generally not transferred. In this case it has been observed that the employees of the cooperative society are here for more than five years and have control over a group of the villagers.

(14). Tractor does not work in condition for more than two years, so common farmers are not getting any benefit from it.

(15). Regular visit and monitoring by district level and state level officers may minimise the corruption.

(16). Strict rules, adherence to rules and timely implementation of the programmes may minimise corruption.

(17). High level corruption is reported in the state and district. Exemplary punishment to concerned officers from top to bottom may have positive impact in minimising corruption.

# Case Observation—3

## Police Stations

Naught police station of Bemtar district. At the entrance there is main veranda in which a big size drum containing roughly 100 litres diesel was kept. Entrance was quite dirty. There is no proper space for officers and constables to sit.

Mr J.S. Sahni is the inspector In-charge of the police station and he has a room to sit and work. Few people from nearby villagers were in the police station. Who said that they were being harassed by the police for no fault?

Dukhu Ram Kotwar of Mau said that he had not been given salary for last four months. His per month salary is Rs 2, 700. He is living on charity given by the villagers.

There are two lock-ups which are small, not as per prescribed norm, no light, no toilet; no water facility is available in the lock-ups.

Mr Omkar Prasad of Mau, a villager was found in the police station with two persons and said that they were beaten by the police in the police station.

The women lock-ups are being used as *malkhana* (store room) for keeping all kind of materials of the police station.

The In-charge of the police station said that they do not keep women in police station, the women are sent to women *thane* in Bilaspur.

## Hirri Police Station

This is one of the police stations. There is one 108 ambulance with a doctor in this police station to help and treat accident patients but the doctors generally remain absent. Generally, they take accident cases to hospital in Bilaspur.

The police station is dirty. A good number of two wheelers, four wheelers, trucks, etc. are lying in the campus of police station.

There is male as well as female lock-ups.

Female lockup is being used as *malkhana* (store room) of the police station. Woman prisoner is sent to woman police station of Bilaspur.

Male lockup is dirty with no light facility, no toilet, no drinking water facility.

## Ratanpur Police Station

This police station is also in Bilaspur, is dirty. No proper space to sit for all the police officers of this police station.

There is only one lock-up for male detainees. Female prisoners are forwarded immediately either to court or to the women police station, Bilaspur.

Mr Sanjeet Kumar/ Shiv Kumar found in the police station. He was sitting outside the lock-up. Lock-up was properly cleaned by Sanjeet Kumar. Sanjeet Kumar was in lock-up last night but since I was visiting so he was kept outside the lock-up. He was detained in the police station because he eloped with a girl who resides next to his house in the village and she is minor, they married in temple. Parents of the girl complained in the police station and so he was caught. According to him, girl's father has old scores to settle with Sanjeet's family, so police caught him and detained him in the lock-up. He said that police scolded him and beat him in the presence of her father.

## Adarsh Kotwali Police Station, Bilaspur

The police station is in Bilaspur town. Police station lock-up is dirty, with no light, no drinking water, no toilet facility.

## Observations

Police station In-charges and others officers have no clarity of the sections under which they should book the accused. No IPC and other allied books were available in any of the visited police stations. If this part is taken care of, think, number of cases can be minimised in courts. Officers of police stations are not aware of the welfare role of police and policing. This input is a must in the present context of the state. It is equally important to sensitise the police officers in human rights.

It has been brought to my notice while I was leaving Raipur that the city SP of Jagdalpur committed suicide after shooting his wife and two children. During my recent visit to Chattisgarh, it has been observed that the city SP of Jagdalpur committed suicide after shooting his wife and children. A day before he was suspended on the pressure of local politics. I was told that before suspending him no show cause notice was issued to him. Recently, he was awarded President medal for meritorious service. A similar incident took place last year in Bilaspur in which the SP of Bilaspur committed suicide.

I think a series of suicide by district level police officers suggest for fresh training input for honest Indian police service officers. The guidelines need to be developed for senior police officers to avoid further suicide.

# Bilaspur, Central Jail

It is one of the oldest jails of India and was established in 1873.The building is quite old. The boundary wall of the jail is close to the halls in which prisoners are lodged. Very recently, two prisoners escaped from this jail through boundary wall. This kind of incident happens in the jail frequently.

Bilaspur jail may be made a heritage jail as many of the freedom fighters were kept in this jail. Bilaspur central jail is overcrowded. Almost three times more than the sanctioned capacities of the jail prisoners are living in the jail. Details are given following:

**(1).** ***Currunt Capisity of the Jail and Prisoners in Jail:*** Capacity of Central jail, Bilaspur is 935 male + 70 women = 1,008 prisoners, currently following numbers of prisoners are in jail:

**Table 7.1** Total Prisoners on 21.02.0201

| *Prisioners* | *Male* | *Foreign Prisoners* | *Third Gender* | *Women* | *Total* |
|---|---|---|---|---|---|
| Hardcore Prisoners | 1,758 | 00 | 01 | 89 | 1,848 |
| General Prisoners | 33 | 00 | 00 | 00 | 33 |
| Under-trail Prisoners | 742 | 01 | 00 | 68 | 811 |
| Civil Prisoners | 03 | 00 | 00 | 00 | 03 |
| Sentence To Death | 01 | 00 | 00 | 00 | 01 |
| Total | 2,537 | 01 | 01 | 157 | 2,696 + 25 Child |

**(2).** ***Under-trail Prisoners:*** There are 742 male and 68 female under-trail prisoners.

**(3).** ***Mentally Sick Prisoners:*** There are 48 mentally sick prisoners.

**(4).** ***Foreign National Prisoners:*** There is one foreign national under-trail prisoner, Victor, from Nigeria.

**(5).** ***Prisioners of the Other State:*** There are 77 under-trail prisoners and 71convicted prisoners in the jail.

**(6).** ***Such Mentally Sick Prisoners who has been Released:*** There are none as such mentally sick prisoners.

**(7).** ***Mentally Sick Prisoners:*** There are 48 sick prisoners.

**(8).** ***Video Conferencing Facility:*** It is available in the jail.

**(9).** **Water and Cleanliness:** Four tube-wells are available for prisoners. Three tube-wells are working. There is one overhead tank from which prisoners get safe drinking water. Municipal corporation cleans time to time overhead water tanker of 2,000 litres. There are five staff to keep the jail clean who work round the clock.

**(10). *Food Arrengement:*** Food is prepared by prisoners as per jail manual. Doctor tastes the food and then it is distributed to prisoners.

**(11). *Non Govermental Observers of Jail:*** As per order dated-16. 11. 2011 of Chhattisgarh Government following are observers.

(1). Mr Manoj Dube, Sirgitee.

(2). Mr Kamlesh Giri Goswami (Advocate, Chunchunia, Sargawa).

(3). Mr Ramanuj Sriwas, Mastoori.

(4). Mr Rajendra Agrhari, Matiyari Sipat.

(5). Mr Narayan Tawarkar, Madhaya Nagariya Chowk, Bilaspur.

(6). Mr Shree Mitra, Vidhaya Nagar, Near Gyatri Mandir, Bilaspur.

(7). Mrs Sarojani Kurmi, Sipat Road Sarkanda, Bilaspur.

**(12). *Women Prisoners:*** There are 157 women prisioners in central jail, Bilaspur.

**(13). *Women Prisoners With Child:*** Following is the details of women prisioners living with children:

**Table 7.2**

| S No | Child Name | Age | Sex | Mother's Name |
|---|---|---|---|---|
| 1. | Krish | 4.5 Years | Male | Smt Premlata |
| 2. | Bikram | 5.5 Years | Male | Smt Rajkumari |
| 3. | Kalpana | 5.5 Years | Female | Smt Dhanabai |
| 4. | Sapna | 3.5 Years | Female | Smt Manisha |
| 5. | Sadhana | 2.58 Years | Female | Smt Bisahin (Grand Mother) |
| 6. | Lucky | 2.5 Years | Male | Smt Kumari (Grand Mother) |
| 7. | Krishna | 2.5 Years | Male | Smt Sangeeta |
| 8. | Anushka | 4 Years | Female | Smt Santoshi |
| 9. | Neha | 4 Years | Female | Smt Teejmati |
| 10. | Mayank | 2.5 Years | Male | Smt Vandana |
| 11. | Arti | 5.5 Years | Female | Smt Nira |
| 12. | Anjali | 2.5 Years | Female | Smt Nira |

| 13. | Kamlesh | 6 YEars | Male | Smt Shayamabai |
|---|---|---|---|---|
| 14. | Karan | 5 Years | Male | Smt Shayamabai |
| 15. | Priyanka | 5 Years | Female | Smt Radha Devi |
| 16. | Chotu | 3 Years | Male | Smt Radhadevi |
| 17. | Aushi | 1.5 Years | Female | Smt Heeme Ekka |
| 18. | Akanksha | 2 Years | Female | Smt Anjali |
| 19. | Diksha | 1 Year | Female | Smt Kuwariya Bai |
| 20. | Chanchal | 1 Year | Female | Smt Kalayani |
| 21. | Ruchi | 1 Year | Female | Smt Gitabai |
| 22. | Nilkhant | 1 Year | Male | Smt Jamuni Bai |
| 23. | Durgeshwari | 14 Month | Female | Smt Lilabai |
| 24. | Gopal | 5 Month | Male | Smt Durga |
| 25. | Gitanjali | 2 Month | Female | Smt Reshma |

**14.** ***All Family was Prisoners:*** None.

**15.** ***Death in Jail:*** None.

**16.** ***Voilane in Jail:*** None.

**17.** ***Staff of the Jail:*** Following are details:

**Table 7.3** Central Jail Staff: Bilaspur

| *Sl No* | *Desiganation* | *Sanction Post* | *Field Up Post* | *Vacant Post* |
|---|---|---|---|---|
| 1. | Jail Superintendent | 1 | 1 | 5 |
| 2. | Medical Officers (Full time) | 1 | 1 | - |
| 3. | Law Officer | 1 | - | - |
| 4. | Deputy Jail Superintendent | 2 | 1 | 1 |
| 5. | Asst. Jail Superintendent | 16 | 5 | 1 |
| 6. | Senior Welfare Officers | 1 | - | 11 |
| 7. | Probation Officers | 1 | 1 | 1 |
| 8. | Deputy Superintendent, | 1 | 1 | - |
| 9. | Senior Insceptor, Weaving | 1 | - | - |
| 10. | Senior Inspector, Training | 1 | 1 | 1 |
| 11. | Tailor Instructor | 1 | 1 | - |
| 12. | Carpentor Inspector | 1 | - | - |
| 13. | Weaving Inspector | 1 | - | 1 |
| 14. | Accountant | 2 | - | 1 |
| 15. | Asstt Grade .II | 1 | 1 | 2 |
| 16. | Asstt Grade .III | 1 | - | - |
| 17. | Press Foremen | 1 | - | 1 |
| 18. | Press Machine Man | 1 | - | 1 |
| 19. | Press Compositer | 1 | - | 1 |

| | | | | |
|---|---|---|---|---|
| 20. | Lab Techinition | 1 | - | 1 |
| 21. | Pharmasist Grade .II | 3 | 2 | 1 |
| 22. | Teacher | 1 | 1 | 1 |
| 23. | Matron | 1 | 1 | - |
| 24. | Head Counstable | 2 | - | - |
| 25. | Head Counstable | 16 | 16 | 2 |
| 26. | Counstable | 125 | 41 | - |
| 27. | Reserve Guard | 1 | 1 | 84 |
| 28. | Reserve Guard | 4 | - | - |
| 29. | Physical Instruct | 1 | - | 4 |
| 30. | Driver Senior Grade | 1 | 1 | 1 |
| 31. | Driver Junior Grade | 1 | 1 | - |
| 32. | Peon | 2 | 2 | - |
| 33. | Sweper | 5 | 5 | - |
| 34. | Data Entry Operator | 1 | - | - |
| 35. | Nurse | 1 | - | 1 |
| | **Total** | **202** | **84** | **118** |

**(18). *Present Security System:*** The officers and guard keep 24 hours watch on prisoners and jail. They change their duty as per specified hours.

**(19). *Payrole:*** 177 prisoners of central jail availed the facility of payroll by 20-13-2014.

**(20). *New Facility:*** None.

**(21). *Doctor in Jail:*** There is one sanction post of doctor in the jail in which a doctor is working.

**(22). *Education:*** The details are following:

**Table 7.4**

| ***Class*** | ***Enrolment Number*** | | ***Total*** |
|---|---|---|---|
| | ***Female*** | ***Male*** | |
| First | 16 | 28 | 44 |
| Second | 08 | 23 | 31 |
| Third | 06 | 21 | 27 |
| Fourth | 03 | 29 | 32 |
| Fifth | 02 | 31 | 33 |
| Sixth | 05 | 30 | 35 |
| Seventh | 03 | 19 | 22 |
| Eighth | 02 | 25 | 27 |
| **Total** | **45** | **206** | **251** |

**Details of Higher Education**

1. BA first – 04 prisioners.
2. BCom Third – 01 prisioners.
3. BA Third – 02 prisioners.
4. MBA first – 05 prisioners.

   Total - 12 prisioners.

**Table 7.5 Education through Indra Gandhi Open University**

| *Male prisoners* | *Female prisoners* | *Total* |
|---|---|---|
| 402 | 63 | 465 |

**Table 7.6 Education under Literacy Programme**

| *Male prisoners* | *Female prisoners* | *Total* |
|---|---|---|
| 202 | 25 | 227 |

**(24).** ***Entertainment:*** TV, Carom, Cheses, Ludo, Daily Newspaper, Magazine are available for intertoinment for prisioners.

**(25).** ***Legal Aid:*** Legal aid is available in the jail by legal literacy camp as well as there is a legal aid clinic.

**(26).** ***NGO:*** None.

**(27).** ***VOCATIONAL TRAINING:*** In order to take the prisoners in mainstream and to rehabilitate they are trained in offset printing press, screen printing, washing powder industries, sewing industries, craft, still furniture, candle making, terracota training, etc.

The female prisoners are trained in making paper, pickle, sewing, candle making, etc. so that after getting released they can lead a normal social life.

**(28).** ***VISIT BY OFFICERS:***

**Table 7.7**

| *Sl No* | *Visiters Name And Position* | *Visit Date* |
|---|---|---|
| 1. | Mr Girdhari Nayak (IPS<br>General Jail and Correctional Servises, Raipur | 04.01.2013 |
| 2. | Mr Girdhari Nayak (IPS<br>General Jail and Correctional Servises, Raipur | 16.02.2013 |
| 3. | Mr B.P. Choudhary<br>DIG Jail and Correctional Servises, Raipur | 27.02.2013 |
| 4. | Mr Girdhari Nayak (IPS<br>General Jail and Correctional Servises, Raipur | 06.03.2013 |
| 5. | Mr Girdhari Nayak (IPS<br>General Jail and Correctional Servises, Raipur | 23.04.2013 |

| | | |
|---|---|---|
| 6. | Mr Thakur Ramsingh, District Magistrate, Bilaspur<br>Mr NK Tekaam, Additional District Magistrate, Bilaspur | 18.05.2013 |
| 7. | Mr Girdhari Nayak (IPS<br>General Jail and Correctional Servises, Raipur | 14.06.2013 |
| 8. | Mr Girdhari Nayak (IPS<br>General Jail and Correctional Servises, Raipur | 03.07.2013 |
| 9. | Mr Gautam Chaurasia, District And Sessions Judge, Bilaspur<br>Mr Minas Naidu, Additional And Sessions Judge<br>Mr Omprakash Chauhan, Chief Judicial Magistrate | 23.06.2013 |
| 10. | Mr Thakur Ramsingh, District Magistrate, Bilaspur<br>Mr RL Dangi, Supretendent of Police,<br>Mr Ranveer Sharma, Additional,<br>Mr Sanjay Kannauje, SDM | 30.06.2013 |
| 11. | Mr Girdhari Nayak (IPS<br>General Jail and Correctional Servises, Raipur | 03.07.2013 |
| 12. | Mr Sunil Kuman Sinha, Judge, Chhattisgarh Hight Court and State Leal Authority, Bilaspur | 28.08.2013 |
| 13. | Mr Gautam Chaurasia, District and Sessions Judge, Bilaspur<br>Mr SK Sipal, Chairaman, State Legal Authority<br>Mr Omprakash Chauhan, Chief Judicial Magistrate | 28.08.2013 |
| 14. | Mr KK Gupta, DIG Jail Correctional Servises, Raipur | 16/17.09.2013 |
| 15. | Prof S. Narayan, Special Rappourter, NHRC, New Delhi<br>Mr LL Ratre, Commisner In-charge, Sabhang, Bilaspur | 18.09.2013 |
| 16. | Mr Thakur Ramsingh, District Magistrate, Bilaspur<br>Mr B N Meena S.P, Bilaspur<br>Mr. J.R Thakur, Additioanl S.P, Bilaspur<br>Miss Madhulika Singh, CSP Civil Line, Bilaspur,<br>Mr Harish Yadav, CSP, Kotawali, Bilaspur | 01.10.2013 |
| 17. | Mr Girdhari Nayak (IPS<br>General Jail and Correctional Servises, Raipur | 14.11.2013 |
| 18. | Mr SL. Ratre Commisiner In-charge, Sambhang, Bilaspur | 26.12.2013 |
| 19. | Mr Rajesh Mishra, IG, Police, Bilaspur Range, Bilaspur<br>Mr Thakur Ramsingh, District Magistrate, Bilaspur<br>Mr NK Tekan Additional Magistrate, Bilaspur<br>Mr BN Meena, S.P , Bilapur<br>Mr SR Thakur Additional SP, Bilaspur | 24.01.2014 |

| | | |
|---|---|---|
| 20. | Dr KK Gupta DIG, Jail and Correctional Service, Bilaspur | 24.01.2014 |
| 21. | Mr Sidhart Komal Singh (IPS Magistrate and District Magistrate , Bilaspur | 20.02.2014 |

**(29). *Meeting With Visitors:*** None.

**(30). *Security Inside Jail:*** The officers and guard of the jail keep vigil and security 24 hours.

**(31). *Inspection:*** Following are the information of inspection.

**Table 7.8**

| ***Sl. No*** | ***Visiters Name And Position*** | ***Visit Date*** |
|---|---|---|
| 1. | Mr Girdhari Nayak (IPS General Jail and Correctional Servises, Raipur Chhatissgarh | 04.01.2013 |
| 2. | Mr Girdhari Nayak (IPS General Jail and Correctional Servises, Raipur Chhatissgarh | 16.02.2013 |
| 3. | Mr BP Choudhary DIG, Jail and Correctional Servises, Raipur | 27.02.2013 |
| 4. | Mr Girdhari Nayak (IPS General Jail and Correctional Servises, Raipur Chhatissgarh | 06.03.2013 |
| 5. | Mr Girdhari Nayak (IPS General Jail and Correctional Servises, Raipur Chhatissgarh | 23.04.2013 |
| 6. | Mr Thakur Ramsingh, District Magistrate, Bilaspur<br>Mr. N.K.Tekaam, Additional District Magistrate, Bilaspur | 18.05.2013 |
| 7. | Mr Girdhari Nayak (IPS General Jail and Correctional Servises, Raipur Chhatissgarh | 14.06.2013 |
| 8. | Mr Girdhari Nayak (IPS General Jail and Correctional Servises, Raipur Chhatissgarh | 03.07.2013 |
| 9. | Mr Gautam Chaurasia, District And Sessions Judge, Bilaspur<br>Mr Minas Naidu, Additional Sessions Judge<br>Mr Omprakash Chauhan, Chief Judicial Magistrate | 23.06.2013 |
| 10. | Mr Thakur Ramsingh, District Magistrate, Bilaspur<br>Mr RL Dangi, Supretendent of Police<br>Mr Ranveer Sharma, Additional,<br>Mr Sanjay Kannauje, SDM | 30.06.2013 |

| | | |
|---|---|---|
| 11. | Mr Girdhari Nayak (IPS<br>General Jail and Correctional Servises, Raipur Chhatissgarh | 03.07.2013 |
| 12. | Mr Sunil Kuman Sinha, Judge,<br>Chhattisgarh Hight Court and State Leal Authority, Bilaspur | 28.08.2013 |
| 13. | Mr Gautam Chaurasia, District and Sessions Judge, Bilaspur<br>Mr SK Sipal, Chairaman, State Legal Authority<br>Mr Omprakash Chauhan, Chief Judicial Magistrate | 28.08.2013 |
| 14. | Mr KK Gupta, DIG, Jail Correctional Servises, Raipur Chhattisgarh, | 16/17.09.2013 |
| 15. | Prof S Narayan, Special Rappourter, NHRC, New Delhi<br>Mr LL Ratre, Commisner In-charge Sabhang, Bilaspur | 18.09.2013 |
| 16. | Mr Thakur Ramsingh, District Magistrate, Bilaspur<br>Mr BN Meena, SP, Bilaspur<br>Mr JR Thakur Additioanl SP, Bilaspur<br>Miss Madhulika Singh, CSP Civil Line, Bilaspur,<br>Mr Harish Yadav, CSP, Kotawali, Bilaspur | 01.10.2013 |
| 17. | Mr Girdhari Nayak (IPS<br>General Jail and Correctional Servises, Raipur Chhatissgarh | 14.11.2013 |
| 18. | Mr SL Ratre, Commisiner In-charge, Sambhang, Bilaspur | 26.12.2013 |
| 19. | Mr Rajesh Mishra, IG Police, Bilaspur Range Bilaspur<br>Mr Thakur Ramsingh, District Magistrate, Bilaspur<br>Mr NK Tekan, Additional Magistrate, Bilaspur<br>Mr BN Meena, S.P , Bilaspur<br>Mr SR Thakur Additional S.P, Bilaspur | 24.01.2014 |
| 20. | Dr KK Gupta, DIG Jail and Correctional Service, Bilaspur | 24.01.2014 |
| 21. | Mr Sidhart Komal Singh (IPS<br>Magistrate and District Magistrate , Bilaspur | 20.02.2014 |

**(32). *Release of Prisoners Before Conclusion of Sentence Period:*** None.

**(33). *Construction of Jail:*** None.

**(34). *Classification of Prisonsrs:*** 00

| **Table 7.9** | | | | | |
|---|---|---|---|---|---|
| ***Prisoners*** | ***Male*** | ***Foreigner Prisoners*** | ***Third Gender*** | ***Female*** | ***Total*** |
| Hardcore Prisoners | 1,758 | 00 | 01 | 89 | 1,848 |
| General Prisoners | 33 | 00 | 00 | 00 | 33 |
| Under Trail Prisoners | 742 | 01 | 00 | 68 | 811 |
| Civil Prisoners | 03 | 00 | 00 | 00 | 03 |
| Sentence To Death | 01 | 00 | 00 | 00 | 01 |
| **Total** | **2,537** | **01** | **01** | **157** | **2,696 + 25 Child** |

**(35).** ***Condition of Prisoners:*** The condition of prisoners is normal and simple.

**(36).** ***Avilability of Electricity In Jail:*** Electricity is always available in the jail.

**(37).** ***Library:*** There is one library containing all kinds of books, including religious books.

**(38).** **Yoga**: Prisoners are giving training in *yoga* in jail.

**(39).** **Lok Adalat And Legal Advice**: On each Saturday Lok Adalat is organised in the jail and legal aid is given to the prisoners.

**(40).** ***Budget:***

**Table 7.10 CENTRAL JAIL BILASPUR**

| | **PARTICULARS** | **BUDGET OF JAIL** |
|---|---|---|
| 1. | Salary | 3,31,45,557.00 |
| 2. | Festival Advance | 9,00,000.00 |
| 3. | Grainary Advance | 2,00,000.00 |
| 4. | Travelling Allowance | 1,03,000.00 |
| 5. | Office Expendicture | 26,43,785.00 |
| 6. | Rent | 25,000.00 |
| 7. | Stationary | 5,81,02,307.00 |
| 8. | Store and Raw Material | 45,00,000.00 |
| 9. | Transport Charges | 19,090.00 |
| 10. | Security Expendicture | 65,000.00 |

| 11. | Security Expendicture | 000 |
|---|---|---|
| 12. | Security Expendicture | 000 |
| 13. | Machine | 4,29,750.00 |
| 14 | Minor Construction | 96,800.00 |
| **Total** | | **10,02,30,289.00** |

**(41).** ***Death in Jail:*** None.

**(42).** ***Small Scale Industry and Cottage Industry:*** The prisoners in the jail are given training in offset printing press, screen printing, washing powder industry, sewing industry, craft, steel furniture, spices, nylon, rope, terracota, candle making Women prisoners are specially trained in paper making, pickle making, sewing, candle making, etc.

**(43).** ***Interview:*** None.

**(44).** ***Cow Herd:*** Yes.

**(45).** ***Garden:*** No.

**(46).** ***Cultural Programme:*** On each religious festival , cultural programme is presented by prisoners.

**(47).** ***Sports:*** Prisoners play indoor games.

**(48).** ***Religious Activities:*** Prisoners are allow to worship their Gods and ditties as per their faith.

**(49).** ***TV and Newspaper:*** Yes.

## Observations

It is evident from the above said tables that central jail, Bilaspur is overcrowded, almost three times more than its capacity.

Proper toilets and drinking water inside the halls in which prisoners and under-trails are kept deserve consideration. Toilets are dirty and drinking water is kept inside plastic buckets. In my last report I mentioned that there were plastic buckets filled with water and also earthen pots were kept outside the hall and in this visit it was found that these buckets were now kept inside the hall. Merely change in place of keeping buckets are not going to provide convicts and under-trials safe drinking water.

Women jail inmate said that they want female legal officers in this jail so that they may share their problems with her frankly. They said they are unable to share their problem with male legal officers at the top of this post of legal officers is lying vacant in this jail.

There are 202 different sanctioned posts in this jail out of which only 84 are filled, remaining 118 posts are vacant. Among vacant posts are Deputy jail superintendent, and Assistant jail superintendent which are essential posts to run the jail systematically and scientifically, this deserves attention of the Commission.

There are 48 mentally sick prisoners in this jail but there is no psychiatrist in this jail. This deserves attention of the Commission.

The prisoners, especially the under-trail prisoners were demanding for their right to vote in elections. They said that when under-trail politicians can contest election then why they are being denied their right to vote.

The board of the Bilaspur central jail does not meet regularly.

A Nigerian prisoner said that there is lack of coordination between jail authorities and police administration because man times he could not be produced in the court in the absence of police. Lack of coordination between jail authorities, police and district administration deserve Commission's attention.

The vocational programmes run by the jail need to be closely monitored to enable the prisoners to draw 'real' benefits from these programmes.

## Juvenile Home, Bilaspur

This juvenile home was established in 1982. Children of Bilaspur, Champa, Korba, Mungeli and Jangir are kept here.

Inmates are kept on the first floor. Training of the inmates is also done on the first floor. Office, kitchen, board room, etc are housed in the ground floor.

### Observation Home of Bilaspur

**(1).** ***Establishment:*** Established under juvenile Act, 2000 and run by *panchyat* and social welfare department. Child below 18 years live here on the order of juvenile judicial board. Children below 18 years of age live here until the order of their release passed by the court.

**(2).** ***Condition of the Building:*** Building of the NGO in which offices are also located. Under the Juvenile Act, 2000 children are allocated rooms to sleep. Kitchen is in the campus and the juvenile court is also in the campus. Considering the security, the house master, trainers, matron, security guards live in the campus.

(3). ***Juvenile Board:*** Principal magistrate of the juvenile board and members execute the work of the juvenile board. 1,221 cases were pending in January, 2014.

(4). ***Medical:*** A part time doctor Dr BR Nanda is currently there to check the health status of the inmates.

(5). ***Food:*** Inmates are served food, tea and breakfast. Special food is served on festivals. The expenditure of the food is borne by the government.

(6). ***Cloth and Bed:*** The inmates get three pair of dress and towel and blanket, bed sheet, pillow as bed.

(7). ***Education:*** The inmates are given vocational training and are taught from 5th to 8th class books as prescribed by boards. Two teachers are appointed by the government to teach the inmates.

(8). ***Training:*** Vocational training is given inmates.

(9). ***Sports and Recreation:*** Annual sports are organised and there is colour TV, CD player, caram board, ludo, Chinese checker, etc. for recreation.

(10) ***Staff and Inmates:*** Following are the staff of the juvenile home:

**Table 7.10**

| ***Sl. No*** | ***Designation*** | ***Name of Staff*** | ***Postyed in Office*** |
|---|---|---|---|
| 1. | In-charge | Mrs C Chandcar | 08.08.2012 |
| 2. | Administrative In-charge | Mr SM Trimothi | 08.08.2012 |
| 3. | Provation | Mr SM Trimothi | 09.09.2008 |
| 4. | Counceller | Mr GL Chowhan | 09.09.2008 |
| 5. | Accountant | Mr US Dube | 09.08.2011 |
| 6. | Matron | None | |
| 7. | Teacher | Mrs Sita Tiwari | 03.08.2010 |
| 8. | Trained | None | |
| 9. | House Master | Mrs Sarswati Rame Shree | 13.10.2008 |
| 10 | Assistant | Mr Deepak Kuman Marco | 30.08.2011 |
| 11 | Peon | Mr Ramsharan Tiwati | 21.06.2001 |
| 12. | Cook | Mrs Binda Tiwari | 15.05.1985 |
| 13. | Cook | Mrs Lata Patel | 20.06.2008 |
| 14. | Care Taker | Mr Tirath Ram | 23.07.2005 |
| 15. | ---------------- | Mrs Kumari Bai | 01.08.2006 |
| 16. | ---------------- | Mr Jagjeevan Das Mahant | 05.07.2005 |
| 17. | Guard | Mr Manoj Kumar Dagir | 20.06.2008 |

| 18. | Gardener | None | |
|---|---|---|---|
| 19. | Swiper | Mr Manish Kumar (Collector) | 24.112010 |
| 20. | Cleaner | Mr Murli Nirmalkar (Colloctor) | 29.08.2011 |
| 21. | Part Time Doctor | Dr BR Nanda | 30.10.1998 |

**Superintendent, Observation Home, Bilaspur**
**Adminision and Release of Child**

**40 Children are in Observation Name**

| Graph 7.1 According To Crime | | | Graph 7.2 Following Are Details Of Children | | | |
|---|---|---|---|---|---|---|
| 1. | Murder | 15 Child | Bilaspur | Mugli | Korwa | Janjagir Champa |
| 2. | Theif | 14 Child | 25 | 06 | 06 | 03 |
| 3. | Rapiest | 10 Child | | | | |
| 4. | Others | 01 Child | | | | |
| | **Total** | **40 Child** | | | | |

Graph 7.3 Allow To Period

| **Less Than 3 Month** | **3 To 6 Month** | **6 Month To 1 Year** | **More Than 1 Year** |
|---|---|---|---|
| 20 | 06 | 05 | 09 |

Graph 7.4 AGE WISE CLASSIFICATION

| 6 TO 9 | 3 TO 6 | 13 TO 16 | 16 TO 18 |
|---|---|---|---|
| 0 | 01 | 08 | 20 |

**(11).** ***Others:*** All required facilities are provided to the inmates as per rule. The inmates are given family environment. Social institutions visit inmates on festive days and organise programmes of the recreation and development for the inmates. The inmates are trained to leave bad habits and to adopt good habits and also to independence and self-independence.

**(12).** ***Wants:*** Staff quarters are required in the campus for the security and safety of the inmates. A vacant post to be filed in urgently shows that teaching and training can be done in time. During rainny season the inmates face problems due to lack of drainage. The municipal commission is requested to take necessary action for drainage.

**Table 7.10** Office of Superintendent, Observation Home, Food

| Per Child/day | | |
|---|---|---|
| ***Sl No*** | ***Name of Things*** | ***Fixed Quantaty*** |
| 1. | Wheat | 300 Gm |
| 2. | Rice | 300 Gm |
| 3. | Dal | 100 Gm |
| 4. | Other Dal | 100 Gm |
| 5. | Vegetable | 300 Gm |
| 6. | Breakfast | 50 Gm |
| 7. | Oil | 20 To 30 Gm |
| 8. | spice | 10 Gm |
| 98. | Milk | 50 Gm |
| 10. | Salt | 15 Gm |
| 11. | Tea | 05 Gm |
| 12. | Suger | 25 Gm |
| 13. | Gas | As Per Necessity |
| 14. | Toothpaste | 50 Gm |
| 15. | Hair Oil | 100 Gm |
| 16. | Bathing Soap | Daily |
| 17. | Washing Soap | Daily |

**Table 7.11** Cloths And Dresses

| ***Sl No*** | ***Details Of Cloths*** | ***Number*** | ***Per Year*** |
|---|---|---|---|
| 1. | Half Pant | 3 | Per Year |
| 2. | Half Shirt | 3 | Per Year |
| 3. | Underwear | 4 | Per Year |
| 4. | Underwear | 4 | Per Year |
| 5. | Towel | 2 | Per Year |
| 6. | Bedsheet | 3 | Per Year |
| 7. | Bedding | 1 | Per 3 Year |
| 8. | Bedding | 1 | Per 3 Year |
| 9. | Pillow | 1 | Per Year |
| 10. | Blanket | 1 | Per Year Winter Season |
| 11 | Woolen Shweter | 1 | Per Year Winter Season |

## Observations

(1). Interacted in depth with two inmates Mr Shivnath Patel, aged 17 years of Pendra and Neeku Kashayap of the same age group, are here for about last two years and are tried under IPC 302.

Both of them told that child trafficking is common at this centre.

(2). Inmates of the juvenile home are not happy with the food being served to them.
(3). Safe drinking water and toilets deserve attention.
(4). Vocational and training programmes ought to be designed according to 'felt need' and notes the routined one.
(5). Juvenile home, Bilaspur may kindly be placed under the direct control of the district magistrate and an executive magistrate be posted here at least for 2 years to improve it because judicial magistrate is over-burdened with judicial work and feel difficulty in giving time to juvenile home.

## Destitute Children Home under JJB, CWC, Bilaspur District

The In-charge of this home said child trafficking is very high in this district. Pendra happens to be a city in which highest trafficking of child takes place. Only girl children ranging between two years to eighteen years were found in this centre.

## Observations

Generally, girls living in this home are unhappy and have all kinds of complain/request.

(1). Education/vocational programme may be designed as per the 'real need' and aspirations.
(2). Food should be nutritious, healthy and seasonal.
(3). There should be proper and timely cooperation and coordination in different departments/wings of the district administration in the interest of an efficient children home.
(4). The In-charge of the home should be active and motherly.

## Health in Bilaspur

I visited Chhattisgarh Institute of Medical Science. Dr R Thakkar, retired from army medical core, joined here as director only last week. Head of the department in surgery and head of nursing were with me during my visit. CIMS was inaugurated in 2001. This was a district hospital before getting it converted to CIMS.

Ten Batches has passed out.

They have difficulty in getting internship as there is no PG course in CIMS.

**Table 7.12 List Of Bounded Labour Found From Kota, 2000 to 2013**

**Year 2000**

| Sl. No | Sl. No. | Name of The Freed Bounded Labourer/Father Name/Husband Name | Date of Freedam | Place | Police Station | District | Fund Spent for Freeing Bounded Labour | Want for Rehabilitation | Name of the Farmer/ Name of the Employer |
|---|---|---|---|---|---|---|---|---|---|
| 1. | 1. | Saroj Kumar, Son of Sonchandra | 08-02-2000 | Ghoghra | Kota | Bilaspur | ------------- | ------------- | Baba, Bribas Field, Gorcha Jul, Unnab |
| 2. | 2. | Sunita Wife of Saroj Kumar | 08-02-2000 | Ghoghra | Kota | Bilaspur | ------------- | ------------- | ------------- |
| 3. | 3. | Smt Pyari Bai Wife of Molu | 08-02-2000 | Jogipur | Kota | Bilaspur | ------------- | ------------- | ------------- |
| 4. | 4. | Smt Kumari Bai Wife of Bhulaw | 08-02-2000 | Jogipur | Kota | Bilaspur | ------------- | ------------- | ------------- |
| 5. | 5. | Mohan Son of Bhalu | 08-02-2000 | Jogipur | Kota | Bilaspur | ------------- | ------------- | ------------- |
| 6. | 6. | Sukhdeo Son of Bhulaw | 08-02-2000 | Jogipur | Kota | Bilaspur | ------------- | ------------- | ------------- |
| 7. | 7. | Smt Kaushalya Wife of Lakshmiram | 08-02-2000 | Jogipur | Kota | Bilaspur | ------------- | ------------- | ------------- |
| 8. | 8. | Smt Kamlesh Wife of Bablu | 08-02-2000 | Jogipur | Kota | Bilaspur | ------------- | ------------- | ------------- |
| 9. | 9. | Kumari Sarswati Daughter of Bholuram | 08-02-2000 | Jogipur | Kota | Bilaspur | ------------- | ------------- | ------------- |
| 10. | 10. | Ashwani Son of Bhulau | 08-02-2000 | Jogipur | Kota | Bilaspur | ------------- | ------------- | ------------- |
| 11. | 11. | Mr Bholu Sion of Lakshmiram | 08-02-2000 | Jogipur | Kota | Bilaspur | ------------- | ------------- | ------------- |
| 12. | 12. | Mr Bhulau Son of Lachiram | 08-02-2000 | Jogipur | Kota | Bilaspur | ------------- | ------------- | ------------- |

| 13. | 13. | Sri Param Son of Kejaram | 08-02-2000 | Ranisagar | Kota | Bilaspur | ------------- | ------------- | ------------- |
|---|---|---|---|---|---|---|---|---|---|
| 14. | 14. | Mr Bhagwat Son of Darshan | 08-02-2000 | Ranisagar | Kota | Bilaspur | ------------- | ------------- | ------------- |
| 15. | 15. | Mr Vijay Kujmar Son of Khagulal | 08-02-2000 | Churput | Kota | Bilaspur | ------------- | ------------- | ------------- |
| 16. | 16. | Mr Shyamlal Son of Vishambhar | 08-02-2000 | Churput | Kota | Bilaspur | ------------- | ------------- | Kanpur, UP |
| 17. | 17. | Mr Durakia Prasad Son of Shyamlal | 08-02-2000 | Churput | Kota | Bilaspur | ------------- | ------------- | ------------- |
| 18. | 18. | Smt Anusuiayabai Husband of Durikaprasad | 08-02-2000 | Churput | Kota | Bilaspur | ------------- | ------------- | ------------- |
| 19. | 19. | Mr Lalji Son of Visharam | 08-02-2000 | Churput | Kota | Bilaspur | ------------- | ------------- | ------------- |
| 20. | 20. | Mr Uttamkumar Son of Lalji | 08-02-2000 | Churput | Kota | Bilaspur | ------------- | ------------- | ------------- |
| 21. | 21. | Smt Guriya Husband of Lalji | 08-02-2000 | Churput | Kota | Bilaspur | ------------- | ------------- | ------------- |
| 22. | 22. | Mr Ashok Kumar Son of Lorikram | 08-02-2000 | Churput | Kota | Bilaspur | ------------- | ------------- | ------------- |
| 23. | 23. | Smt Sujbai Husband of Lorikram | 08-02-2000 | Churput | Kota | Bilaspur | ------------- | ------------- | ------------- |
| 24. | 24. | Mr Shivkumar Son of Makhan | 08-02-2000 | Churput | Kota | Bilaspur | ------------- | ------------- | ------------- |
| 25. | 25. | Smt Shivkumar Husband of Shivkumar | 08-02-2000 | Churput | Kota | Bilaspur | ------------- | ------------- | ------------- |
| 26. | 26. | Mr Dukalpa Son of Sakhiram | 08-02-2000 | Churput | Kota | Bilaspur | ------------- | ------------- | ------------- |
| 27. | 27. | Mr Ramji Son of Alal | 08-02-2000 | Churput | Kota | Bilaspur | ------------- | ------------- | ------------- |

| 28. | 28. | Kumari Nirmala Daughter of Lalji | 08-02-2000 | Churput | Kota | Bilaspur | -------------- | -------------- | -------------- |
|---|---|---|---|---|---|---|---|---|---|
| 29. | 29. | Kumari Ila Daughter of Lorik | 08-02-2000 | Churput | Kota | Bilaspur | -------------- | -------------- | -------------- |
| 30. | 30. | Mr Ravi Son of Lorik | 08-02-2000 | Churput | Kota | Bilaspur | -------------- | -------------- | -------------- |
| 31. | 31. | Mr Santosh Son of Lorik | 08-02-2000 | Churput | Kota | Bilaspur | -------------- | -------------- | -------------- |
| 32 | 32 | Kumari Kala Daughter of Lorik | 08-02-2000 | Churput | Kota | Bilaspur | -------------- | -------------- | -------------- |
| 33. | 33. | Mr Rajkumar Son of Bhadwariya | 08-02-2000 | Sirisiha | Kota | Bilaspur | -------------- | -------------- | Pratap Nagar, Pal Rajpal, I Udyog, Ganga Ganj, Thana-Harchandrapur, Distt. Raibaraeli. UP |
| 34. | 34. | Mr Bala Son of Baglu | 08-02-2000 | Mudhipar | Kota | Bilaspur | -------------- | -------------- | -------------- |
| 35. | 35. | Mr Jagdish Son of Sawan | 08-02-2000 | Kushpatti | Kota | Bilaspur | -------------- | -------------- | -------------- |
| 36. | 36. | Mr Manohar Son of Sateru | 08-02-2000 | Murtipara | Kota | Bilaspur | -------------- | -------------- | -------------- |
| 37. | 37. | Mr Daisai Son of Santosh | 08-02-2000 | Mohadi | Kota | Bilaspur | -------------- | -------------- | -------------- |
| 38. | 38. | Mr Rupbandi Son of Hakhararam | 08-02-2000 | Podhi | Kota | Bilaspur | -------------- | -------------- | -------------- |
| 39. | 39. | Mrs Yaousada Wife of Lakhan | 08-02-2000 | Kota | Kota | Bilaspur | -------------- | -------------- | -------------- |
| 40. | 40. | Mrs JamwanTi Wife of Uman | 08-02-2000 | Kota | Kota | Bilaspur | -------------- | -------------- | -------------- |
| 41. | 41. | Mrs Surekha Wife of Lakhan | 08-02-2000 | Kota | Kota | Bilaspur | -------------- | -------------- | -------------- |

| | Year 2003 | | | | | | | | |
|---|---|---|---|---|---|---|---|---|---|
| 42. | 1. | Dilip Kumar Father of Nandaw | Paper No 3882 @ 04-04-2003 | Lalpur | Kota | Bilaspur | ------------- | ------------- | Kausambhi, UP |
| 43. | 2. | Mrs Kachara Bai Wife of Dilip Kumar | ------------- | Lalpur | Kota | Bilaspur | ------------- | ------------- | ------------- |
| 44. | 3. | Kumari Parwati Daughter of DiliP Kumar | ------------- | Lalpur | Kota | Bilaspur | ------------- | ------------- | ------------- |
| 45. | 4. | Mr Vijay Kumar Son of Radhepal | ------------- | Rani Sagar | Kargi Road | Bilaspur | ------------- | ------------- | Suman Vibhra Field, Gram Raj, Post-Basti, Thane-Gauriganj, Janpad, Sultanpur. |
| 46 | 5. | Smt Sunita Bai | ------------- | Rani Sagar | Kargi Road | Bilaspur | ------------- | ------------- | ------------- |
| | **Year 2005** | | | | | | | | |
| 47. | 1. | Smt Mira Husband of Godh | 14-09-2015 | Vill Belgahana Kota | Kota | Bilaspur | ------------- | ------------- | ------------- |
| 48. | 2. | Omkar Father of Umasingh | ------------- | ------------- | Kota | Bilaspur | ------------- | ------------- | ------------- |
| 49. | 3. | Jeet Singh Father of Kamal Singh | ------------- | ------------- | Kota | Bilaspur | ------------- | ------------- | ------------- |
| 50. | 4. | Basant Bai Husband of Jita Singh | ------------- | ------------- | Kota | Bilaspur | ------------- | ------------- | ------------- |
| 51. | 5. | Sunil Father Ganesh Singh | ------------- | ------------- | Kota | Bilaspur | ------------- | ------------- | ------------- |
| 52. | 6. | Sabita Husband of Sunil | ------------- | ------------- | Kota | Bilaspur | ------------- | ------------- | ------------- |

| 53. | 7. | Vikram Father of Narayan Singh | ------------- | ------------- | Kota | Bilaspur | ------------- | ------------- | ------------- |
|---|---|---|---|---|---|---|---|---|---|
| 54. | 8. | Anita Husband of Vikram | ------------- | ------------- | Kota | Bilaspur | ------------- | ------------- | ------------- |
| 55. | 9. | Ajit Father Kamal Singh | ------------- | ------------- | Kota | Bilaspur | ------------- | ------------- | ------------- |
| 56. | 10. | Arti Husband of Ajit Singh | ------------- | ------------- | Kota | Bilaspur | ------------- | ------------- | ------------- |
| 57. | 11. | Sita Father of Kamal Singh | ------------- | ------------- | Kota | Bilaspur | ------------- | ------------- | ------------- |
| 58. | 12. | Sangeeta Husband of sitaram | ------------- | ------------- | Kota | Bilaspur | ------------- | ------------- | ------------- |
| 59. | 13. | Narayan Father of Motilal | ------------- | ------------- | Kota | Bilaspur | ------------- | ------------- | ------------- |
| 60. | 14. | Rekha Husband of Narayan | ------------- | ------------- | Kota | Bilaspur | ------------- | ------------- | ------------- |
| 61. | 15. | Raghuveer Father of Ganesh | ------------- | ------------- | Kota | Bilaspur | ------------- | ------------- | ------------- |
| 62. | 16. | Chotu Father of Ganesh | ------------- | ------------- | Kota | Bilaspur | ------------- | ------------- | ------------- |
| 63. | 17. | Rupkuwar Father of Ramavatar | ------------- | ------------- | Kota | Bilaspur | ------------- | ------------- | ------------- |
| 64 | 18. | Shailendra Father of AmarsIngh | ------------- | ------------- | Kota | Bilaspur | ------------- | ------------- | ------------- |
| 65. | 19. | Bandana Husband of Shailendra | ------------- | ------------- | Kota | Bilaspur | ------------- | ------------- | ------------- |
| 66. | 20. | Gangasingh Father of Amarsingh | ------------- | ------------- | Kota | Bilaspur | ------------- | ------------- | ------------- |

| 67. | 21. | Mr Kameshwar Anant Father of Shivsagar | 30.01.2011 | Gram-Amne, Thana-Kota, Distt-Bilaspur | Kota | Bilaspur | -------------- | -------------- | Meshsarh Maa Bhagwati, Vikra Field, Adilpur, Thane-Jagdishpur, Gauriganj, Chatrapati, Mahuji, Maharajnagar, UP |
|---|---|---|---|---|---|---|---|---|---|
| 68. | 22. | Mrs Sembai Wife of Nageshwar | 30.01.2011 | Gram-Amne, Thana-Kota, Distt-Bilaspur | Kota | Bilaspur | -------------- | -------------- | -------------- |
| 69. | 23. | Gauri Daughetr of Nageshwar | 30.01.2011 | Gram-Amne, Thana-Kota, Distt-Bilaspur | Kota | Bilaspur | -------------- | -------------- | -------------- |
| 70. | 24. | Mr Shivcharan Son of Maheshkumar | 30.01.2011 | Gram-Ghoradih, Thane-Kota, Tatkhtapur, Distt-Bilaspur | Kota | Bilaspur | -------------- | -------------- | -------------- |
| 71. | 25. | Mr Ajjuram Son of Gurucharan | 30.01.2011 | Gram-Ghoradih, Thane-Kota, Tatkhtapur, Distt-Bilaspur | Kota | Bilaspur | -------------- | -------------- | -------------- |
| 72. | 26. | Mr Shivnarayan Son of Devlal | 30.01.2011 | Gram-Ratanpur, Thane-Ratanpur, Bilaspur | Kota | Bilaspur | -------------- | -------------- | -------------- |
| 73. | 27. | Smt Rajeem Wife of Mr Shivram | 30.01.2011 | Gram-Ghoradih, Thane-Kota, Tatkhtapur, Distt-Bilaspur | Kota | Bilaspur | -------------- | -------------- | -------------- |

| | | | | | | | | | |
|---|---|---|---|---|---|---|---|---|---|
| 74. | 28. | Mr Chandraprakash Son of Ramesh | 30.01.2011 | Gram-Semariya, Thane-Kargiroad Kota, Distt Bilaspur. | Kota | Bilaspur | ------------- | ------------- | ------------- |
| 75. | 29. | Smt Deepa Wife of Mr. Chandraprakash | 30.01.2011 | Gram Semariya, Thane-Kargiroad Kota, Distt Bilaspur. | Kota | Bilaspur | ------------- | ------------- | ------------- |
| 76. | 30. | Mr Ramesh Kumar Son of Panchu | 30.01.2011 | Gram Semariya, Thane-Kargiroad Kota, Distt Bilaspur. | Kota | Bilaspur | ------------- | ------------- | ------------- |
| 77. | 31. | Smt Meenabai Wife of Ramesh Kumar | 30.01.2011 | Gram Semariya, Thane-Kargiroad Kota, Distt Bilaspur. | Kota | Bilaspur | ------------- | ------------- | ------------- |
| 78. | 32. | Smt Meena Wife of Shivnarayan | 30.01.2011 | Gram-Ratanpur, Thanne-Ratanpur,Distt Bilaspur. | Kota | Bilaspur | ------------- | ------------- | ------------- |
| 79. | 33. | Smt Sita Wife of Ashok Kumar | 30.01.2011 | Gram Semariya, Thane-Kargiroad Kota, Distt Bilaspur. | Kota | Bilaspur | ------------- | ------------- | ------------- |
| 80. | 34. | Mr Ashok Kumar Son of Panchu | 30.01.2011 | Gram Semariya, Thane-Kargiroad Kota, Distt Bilaspur | Kota | Bilaspur | ------------- | ------------- | ------------- |
| 81. | 35. | Smt Kriti Wife of Tribhanjan | 30.01.2011 | Gram-Mohanbhaj, Thane-Kota, Takhatpur, Distt-Bilaspur | Kota | Bilaspur | ------------- | ------------- | ------------- |

| | | | | | | | | | |
|---|---|---|---|---|---|---|---|---|---|
| 82. | 36. | Smt Jameela Wife of Sonudas | 30.01.2011 | Gram-Mohanbhaj, Thane-Kota, Takhatpur, Distt-Bilaspur | Kota | Bilaspur | ------------- | ------------- | ------------- |
| 83. | 37. | Smt Lakshmibai Wife of Mr. Ghamshayam | 30.01.2011 | Gram-Mohanbhaj, Thane-Kota, Takhatpur, Distt-Bilaspur | Kota | Bilaspur | ------------- | ------------- | ------------- |
| 84. | 38. | Mr Suresh Son of Laher | 30.01.2011 | Gram-Mohanbhaj, Thane-Kota, Takhatpur, Distt-Bilaspur | Kota | Bilaspur | ------------- | ------------- | ------------- |
| 85. | 39. | Smt Lovely Bai Wife of Bodhram | 30.01.2011 | Gram-Mohanbhaj, Thane-Kota, Takhatpur, Distt-Bilaspur | Kota | Bilaspur | ------------- | ------------- | ------------- |
| 86. | 40. | Smt Guddu Wife of Dilchand | 30.01.2011 | Gram-Mohanbhaj, Thane-KOta, Takhatpur, Distt-Bilaspur | Kota | Bilaspur | ------------- | ------------- | ------------- |
| 87. | 41. | Mr Ghamshyam Wife of Paroman | 30.01.2011 | Gram-Mohanbhaj, Thane-Kota, Takhatpur, Distt-Bilaspur | Kota | Bilaspur | ------------- | ------------- | ------------- |

| | | | | | | | | | |
|---|---|---|---|---|---|---|---|---|---|
| 88. | 42. | Mr Sonudas Son of Pritam | 30.01.2011 | Gram-Mohanbhaj, Thane-Kota, Takhatpur, Distt-Bilaspur | Kota | Bilaspur | ------------ | ------------ | ------------ |
| 89. | 43. | Mr Devi Pandey Son of Mahesh Khande | 30.01.2011 | Gram-Ghoghadih, Thane-Kota, Takhtpur, Distt-Bilaspur | Kota | Bilaspur | ------------ | ------------ | ------------ |
| 90. | 44. | Smt Sita Wife of Jaykumar | 30.01.2011 | Gram-Mohanbhaj, Thane-Kota, Takhatpur, Distt-Bilaspur | Kota | Bilaspur | ------------ | ------------ | ------------ |
| 91. | 45. | Mr Dilchand Son of Shivdayal | 30.01.2011 | Gram-Mohanbhaj, Thane-Kota, Takhatpur, Distt-Bilaspur | Kota | Bilaspur | ------------ | ------------ | ------------ |
| 92. | 46. | Mr Chandra Prakash Son of Gupta | 30.01.2011 | Gram-Mohanbhaj, Thane-Kota, Takhatpur, Distt-Bilaspur | Kota | Bilaspur | ------------ | ------------ | ------------ |
| 93. | 47. | Smt Santosh Bai Wife of Devi Khande | 30.01.2011 | Gram-Mohanbhaj, Thane-Kota, Takhatpur, Distt-Bilaspur | Kota | Bilaspur | ------------ | ------------ | ------------ |
| 94. | 48. | Smt Santoshi Wife of Suresh | 30.01.2011 | Gram-Mohanbhaj, Thane-Kota, Takhatpur, Distt-Bilaspur | Kota | Bilaspur | ------------ | ------------ | ------------ |

| | | | | | | | | | |
|---|---|---|---|---|---|---|---|---|---|
| 95. | 49. | Mr Kamta Prasad Son of Nandram | 30.01.2011 | Gram-Mohanbhaj, Thane-Kota, Takhatpur, Distt-Bilaspur | Kota | Bilaspur | ------------- | ------------- | ------------- |
| 96. | 50. | Mr Jaikumar Son of Guha | 30.01.2011 | Gram-Mohanbhaj, Thane-Kota, Takhatpur, Distt-Bilaspur | Kota | Bilaspur | ------------- | ------------- | ------------- |
| 97. | 51. | Mr Bodhuram Son of Nandram | 30.01.2011 | Gram-Mohanbhaj, Thane-Kota, Takhatpur, Distt-Bilaspur | Kota | Bilaspur | ------------- | ------------- | ------------- |
| 98. | 52. | Mr Anandlal Son of Komal Khande | 30.01.2011 | Gram-Mohanbhaj, Thane-Kota, Takhatpur, Distt-Bilaspur | Kota | Bilaspur | ------------- | ------------- | ------------- |
| 99. | 53. | Mr Bablu Son of Mahendra | 30.01.2011 | Gram-Mohanbhaj, Thane-Kota, Takhatpur, Distt-Bilaspur | Kota | Bilaspur | ------------- | ------------- | ------------- |
| 100. | 54. | Kumari Alpana Daughter of Khande | 30.01.2011 | Gram-Mohanbhaj, Thane-Kota, Takhatpur, Distt-Bilaspur | Kota | Bilaspur | ------------- | ------------- | ------------- |
| 101. | 55. | Smt Ranjeeta Wife of Bablu | 30.01.2011 | Gram-Mohanbhaj, Thane-Kota, Takhatpur, Distt-Bilaspur | Kota | Bilaspur | ------------- | ------------- | ------------- |

| | | | | | | | | | |
|---|---|---|---|---|---|---|---|---|---|
| 102. | 56. | Mr Komal KHande Son of Rekharam | 30.01.2011 | Gram-Mohanbhaj, Thane-Kota, Takhatpur, Distt-Bilaspur | Kota | Kota | Bilaspur | ------------- | ------------- |
| 103. | 57. | Smt Punabai Wife of Komal Khande | 30.01.2011 | Gram-Mohanbhaj, Thane-Kota, Takhatpur, Distt-Bilaspur | Kota | Bilaspur | ------------- | ------------- | ------------- |
| 104. | 58. | Smt Melanbai Wife of Kamtaprasad | 30.01.2011 | Gram-Mohanbhaj, Thane-Kota, Takhatpur, Distt-Bilaspur | Kota | Bilaspur | ------------- | ------------- | ------------- |
| 105. | 59. | Mr Khemraj Son of Kamta | 30.01.2011 | Gram-Mohanbhaj, Thane-Kota, Takhatpur, Distt-Bilaspur | Kota | Bilaspur | ------------- | ------------- | ------------- |
| 106. | 60. | Smt Parwati Wife of Khemraj | 30.01.2011 | Gram-Mohanbhaj, Thane-Kota, Takhatpur, Distt-Bilaspur | Kota | Bilaspur | ------------- | ------------- | ------------- |
| 107. | 61. | Smt Satbai Wife of Mahetter | 30.01.2011 | Gram-Podhi, Thane-Kota, Distt-Bilaspur | Kota | Bilaspur | ------------- | ------------- | Distt. Basti, UP |
| 108. | 62. | Mr Sandeep Son of Mahettar | 30.01.2011 | Gram-Podhi, Thane-Kota, Distt-Bilaspur | Kota | Bilaspur | ------------- | ------------- | ------------- |
| 109. | 63. | Parteema Putri Daughter of Maheteer | 30.01.2011 | Gram-Podhi, Thane-Kota, Distt-Bilaspur | Kota | Bilaspur | ------------- | ------------- | ------------- |

## Observations

1. During the visit it has been observed that the hospitals and the wards are dusty, dirty, spitted on the wall everywhere which may lead to infections to the patients.
2. Cleanliness and proper disinfection of the wards and the hospital are essential.
3. While visiting the medical ward it has been observed the indoor patients are advised and forced to buy medicines from outside markets. One Mrs Sushmati wife of Sawan and Mr Radhe Lal told that they bought medicine prescribed by Dr Mrs Yashmin Khan and advised by nurse Mrs Sadhana Jain to by medicine from open market for which Mrs Sushmati said that she sold her gold ring to buy the medicine in the presence of director of Chhattisgarh Institute of Medicals Sciences and HOD surgery of CIMS. The state government has given clear direction that all patients specially the poor patients be given all medicines and diet in the hospital free of cost by the hospital administration.
4. The vacant post of CIMS must be filled in on urgent basis.
5. The hospital should have constructions like *Rain Basera* for the accompaning persons of the patients. This will help in keeping hospital clean.
6. It has been reported that the waiting time from registration to admission in the hospital is almost two hours. In the interest of providing immediate and urgent medical facility this waiting time needs to be minimised.

## Bonded Labour

Bonded labour is present in the district but there is no such list. I tried to find out personally but could not locate. In some villages, *Sarpanch* said that they also know that bonded labour is present but neither the master nor the labourer wants to be identified as bonded labour for obvious reasons. This requires commissioning of a research project on this issue in the state in collaboration with the state government.

## Child Labour

Child labour is a common sight in tea stalls, shops, hotels, agricultural fields etc. Female child labourers freed from their masters are kept in child home. Labour department is doing good job in the field of child labour.

**Pic. 7.1**

## Labour in Unorganised Sector

Mukhya Mantri Kaushal Vikas Yojna is very successful in the district. I visited Sipat Naawa *gaon* of Bilaspur district in which women are trained in sewing, stitching cloths; beautician courses, etc. About 100 women from different villages of this panchyat were present. District labour commissioner was also present during my visit. Mukhya Mantri Kaushal Vikas Yojna has done excellent work which need to be demonstrated outside the state. These women need to be given linkages with other development programmes so that they may get regular income each month. Employment programmes for these women be drafted and implemented.

## List of Bencificiaries and a Case Study

**In the Chhattisgarh unorganized workers state social security division**

- Total Benificiears - 67474
- Distributionj Of Cycle - 4730
- Distribution Of Machine - 400
- Unorganisesd Hawker Cycle Distribution - 500

**Table 7.13 Building and Other Construction Workers Welfare Details Chhattisgarh**

| *Sl No.* | *Name Of Project* | *Boy* | *Girl* | *Total Beneficiaries Number* | *Total Distributed Money* |
|---|---|---|---|---|---|
| 1. | Nanihal Scolarship Distribution Programme | 1,891 | 2,033 | 3,924 | 30,01,600.00 |
| 2. | Delevery Suppport System | | | 570 | 37,36,000.00 |
| 3. | Patriarch Support | | | 246 | 6,93,000.00 |
| 4. | Last Rites Support | | | 138 | 34,55,000.00 |
| 5. | Community Marriege | | | 499 | 60,30,000.00 |
| | **Total** | | | **5,377** | **1,69,15,600.00** |

| **Table 7.14** | | |
|---|---|---|
| Vishwakarma Acciendental Relief Fund | 4 | 210,000.00 |
| Distribution | 4 | 5,013 |
| Ladies Sewing Machine | 4 | 5,000 |
| Kit Distribution | 4 | 9,031 |

**Table 7.15 Benificial of Mukhya Mantri Union Yojna**

| Trade | Education | | | |
|---|---|---|---|---|
| Training | 87 | - | | |
| Sewing Training | 142 | 105 | Contiuning | 120 are Being Instituted |
| Electricion Training | 24 | 102 | To be Instituted | |

Benificiary Of Self Dependent Pention Programme

## Succeesful Story Brick Kiln Female Workers

1. Mr Neeta Prajapati (wife)
   Age: 30 years
   Female labourer in brick klin

2. Sri Prajapati (Husband)
   Brick kiln worker
   Bilaspur

3. Two Children, one son going to school
4. Wife and husband are registered under Chhattisgarh Building Construction Workers Welfare Society and are recipient of facilities provided under this scheme.
5. Mrs Neeta Prajapati got the training of beautician course under this programme.
6. Mrs Neeta Prajapati is of the opinion that the work of brick kiln workers is of seasonal nature and during raineny season they do not get any work. Therefore ,she took training in beautician course from which she earns her livelihood when there is no work in brick kiln. Thus, now with the training in beautician course She is able to earn throughout the year. This has raised her annual income. Children are also getting scholarship for education under this Scheme.

## Land Acquisition and Rehabilitation Programme

Land of 3,101 families was acquired by the state government for NTPC at Sipat, Bilaspur.

Met Assistant general manager, human relations and another Assistant general manager, head of human relations, NTPC in addition to other officials and also to affected population. The affected population have grievances that they have not been properly rehabilitated and promises made by NTPC are not fulfilled.

## NTPC, Sipat, Rehabilitation Programmes

Presentation on Status of Rehabilitation Action Plan and Recruitment of Paps at Ntpc Sipat

### Background

- Under Section 4(1) notification for NTPC Sipat was published on 6/11/1998.
- Socio Economic Survey of all major affected villages was done by llT-Kanpur in 1998.
- Committee comprising *sarpanch and upsarpanch* of all eight villages and other local people was constituted on 28.3.2000 for formulating Rehabilitation Action Plan.
- Another Committee formulated by Collector, Bilaspur 31.3.2000 comprising District Revenue Authorities, Labour,

Employment officer, CEO, district *panchayat,* sociologist and educationist to review the draft RAP and finalisation of RAP.

- District administration has also convened open forum at Bilaspur on 21.4.2000 chaired by Shri SC Behar, Chief Advisor to Hon'ble Chief Minister of MP.
- Follow up review meeting also held by Shri SC Behar on 15.7.2000 where the provisions of draft RAP was further discussed with environmentalist and Paryavaran, an NGO.
- Finally, after series of meeting of two Committees formulated by Collector, Bilaspur, the Rehabilitation Action Plan for NTPC Sipat was finalised on 5.8.2000.

## Sailent Features of RAP

- As per finding of Socio Economic Survey by IIT-Kanpur, 80 per cent of the affected are farmers. Care was taken not to affect a single household (no displacement).
- NTPC Sipat is being installed with environment friendly Super Critical Technology, employment opportunity in NTPC shall be comparatively less.
- In view of 'Land for Land' option was considered as Prime Rehabilitation Measure and care was taken to enable the RAPs to acquire same or more land nearby than that of acquisition. In addition to land compensation, rehabilitation assistance shall be paid. On submission of proof of land purchase, further land registration and development cost shall be paid.

## Status of RAP in 2007

- As per provision of RAP of NTPC, Sipat, the further land acquisition, distribution of compensation, distribution of rehabilitation amount for purchase of land and distribution of land registration amount and land development costs were disbursed.
- It was time to time reviewed by district authority and finally, it was reviewed and recorded in the MOM of meeting of collector, Bilaspur dated 26.02.2007 that all the PAPs were extended rehabilitation assistance as per RAP except few cases beyond control of NTPC (Family dispute/Not traceable, etc).

## Provisions of Employment in RAP

- Sipat project being based on super critical technology, the employment opportunities are comparatively less. Hence 'Land for Land' option has been considered as prime rehabilitation measure.
- For direct employment in unskilled category, only PAPs are to be considered.
- In the skilled category, preference would be given to the RAPs.
- In both the above categories, employment shall be subject to eligibility as per NTPC R and R policy, availability of vacancies, NTPC's recruitment policy and Government policy on reservation.
- The provisions related to 'Employment' as provided in approved Rehabilitation Action Plan (RAP) is as under:
- The basis of extending the preference in employment will be on family basis. The family includes husband, wife and dependent children. The eligibility criteria will be as follows:
- The broader groups of Project Affected Persons (*khatedars*) in order of preference will be as below:

✓ *Group 1*: Those project affected persons (*khatedars*), who are resident of the area and are owners of the acquired land for more than 20 years prior to date of section 4(i) notification of the land Acquisition on Act, 1894.

✓ *Group 2* Those project affected persons (*khatedars*), who are resident of the area and are owners of the acquired land for more than 10 years prior to date of section 4(i) notification.

✓ *Group 3* Those project affected persons (*khatedars*), who are resident of the area and are owners of the acquired land for more than one year prior to date of section 4(i) notification.

- Further, each of the above three groups shall have three sub–groups which shall, in order of group priority, be as below and comprise of:

✓ *Sub–group (a):* Those PAPs (*khatedars*), whose more than 5.0 (Five) acres land is acquired.

✓ *Sub–group (b):* Those PAPs (*khatedars*), whose more than 1.0 (One) acre to (Five) acres land is acquired.

✓ *Sub–group (c):* Those PAPs (*khatedars*), whose less than (One) acre land is acquired.

- In each of the above three sub–groups, the priority list of the PAPs (*khatedars*) shall be prepared in the descending order of the percentage of land acquired out of the total land holding of the respective PAPs (*khatedars*).

## Recruitment in 2007

- Open advertisement issued in Newspaper for recruitment of technical posts like Artisan Trainee, Lab Asstt. Trainee and Diploma Trainee
- As per demand of land oustees, age relaxation for PAPs corrigendum published in newspaper
- However, due to further agitation only PAPs who had applied against open advertisement were considered and total 39 were also recruited. At that time only PAP status was accepted and no other criteria like quantum of land loss/ period of land holding/relation with main *khatedar* or, consent of all *khatedar* etc were not considered

## Brief Status of Recruitment at NTPC, Sipat

- A meeting was organised on 23rd November, 2007 under chairpersonship of Hon'ble Chief Minister, CG. In the meeting Hon'ble Chief Minister asked that a plan for R and R should be submitted within one month.
- Vide letter Ref. 01/CMD/PES/603-141, dated 29.12.2007, NTPC submitted status of R and R plan, and also furnished roadmap of further action(CMD, NTPC to CM–CG).
- On 09.02.2008, a presentation was made by Dir(Proj) on Rehabilitation Action Plan and recruitment status for kind perusal of Hon'ble CM(CG). In the presentation preference has been defined for non executives recruitment as follows:
  - ❖ Land oustees will have the first preference.
  - ❖ Local residents from the Distt. Bilaspur, Korba and Janjgir Champa will have the next preference.
  - ❖ Balance required if any and not available from SI No 1 and 2 above will be taken from the Chhattishgarh State.
  - ❖ In no case any recruitment in Non-executive category will be done from outside the state of CG.
  - ❖ Employment shall be subject to the availability of vacancies, suitability, NTPC recruitment policy and Government. policy on reservation.
- A meeting was held on 21st February 2008 under chairmanship of collector, Bilaspur in which the recruitment plan of 692 Non-executives was discussed. It was also informed that for further recruitment, priority list of the land oustees shall

be prepared as per the RAP-Rehabilitation Action Plan. The details of vacancies declared in 2008 is as below:

- ❖ Diploma/ITI :368
- ❖ Others (Lab Asstt., Asstt general, Asstt F&A, Staff Nurse, Draughtsman, Para medical, Steno, Store keeper, etc) :141
- ❖ Attendant/*Mazdoor* (unskilled) :117
- ❖ Retired Railway driver/ASM :66
- ❖ Total :692

- Recruitment made in 2007 : 39
- Recruitment made since 2008 : 299
- Under ITI training sponsored by NTPC and shall be absorbed after completion of Training : 39
- Requisite percantage of ST candidates are not available in PAPs resulting backlog.
- Non-availability of qualified candidate among PAPs in stenography, staff nurse and draughtsman.

### Priority List

- As per decision taken in the meeting dated 21.02.2008 with collector, Bilaspur and local MLA a priority list consisting of PAPs whose one acre or more land was acquired and the land holding of minimum 20 years prior to section 4(1) notification, i.e 06.11.1998. (This is also in line with provisions of RAP)
- Since 2008, recruitment for various posts and nomination for ITI, Government. ITI Koni has been done only considering PAPs from priority list as per their position and educational qualification as per suitability for various posts.

## Observation

The promises, as claimed by affected population, need careful consideration and must be fulfilled in a time frame else such aspirations lead to Naxalism and Maoism from which the state is already suffering.

# 8
# The World Report of Human Rights

The World Report of Human Rights Watch, 2013 presents its view on the status of human rights in India. We are reproducing the report of Human Rights Watch in larger interest of the people in the following lines:

**India**

India, the world's most populous democracy, continues to have significant human rights problems despite making commitments to tackle some of the most prevalent abuses. The country has a thriving civil society, free media, and an independent judiciary. But longstanding abusive practices, corruption, and lack of accountability for perpetrators foster human rights violations.

Government initiatives, including police reform and improved access to healthcare and education, languish due to poor implementation. Many women, children, *Dalits* (so-called untouchables), tribal communities, religious minorities, people with disabilities, and sexual and gender minorities remain marginalised and continue to suffer discrimination because of government failure to train public officials in stopping discriminatory behaviour.

Impunity remains a serious problem, particularly for abuses committed by security forces in Jammu and Kashmir, the north-east, and areas in central and eastern India facing a Maoist insurgency. Resource extraction and infrastructure projects often have deleterious environmental and economic impacts, and may infringe upon the rights of affected communities.

The Centre Government tightened restrictions on internet content, insisting the measures are to curtail threats to public order. It used a colonial-era sedition law to stifle peaceful dissent in 2012 on issues ranging from the government's handling of the Maoist insurgency and corruption, to protests against a nuclear power plant in the southern state of Tamil Nadu. The protection of religious minorities received a boost from the prosecutions of several suspects in the 2002 Gujarat riots, resulting in over 75 convictions in 2012. These included the conviction of Maya Kodnani, a former minister and a leader of Bajrang Dal, a militant Hindu organisation.

### Impunity

Members of security forces implicated in serious rights abuses continued to enjoy impunity, in large measure due to India's laws and policies.

The Indian defence establishment resisted attempts in 2012 to revoke or revise the Armed Forces Special Powers Act (AFSPA), which permits soldiers to commit serious human rights violations with effective immunity.

### Maoist Insurgency

Maoists operations extend to nine states in central and eastern India, finding support in regions with weak governance, infrastructure and basic public services, such as healthcare and education.

Maoist insurgents known as Naxalites continued to target government schools and hospitals. Paramilitary forces continued to occupy and use schools as bases, despite a Supreme Court order to vacate all schools by May 2011. In September, government officials in Chhattisgarh, central India, stated they would remove forces from 36 schools and hostels because of their impact on children's education.

At this writing, Maoist-related violence in 2012 had resulted in 257 deaths, including 98 civilians. In June, security forces killed 19 villagers in Chhattisgarh state in a night operation, prompting widespread condemnation.

Civil society activists in Maoist areas remain increasingly at risk from both Maoists and state security forces. Many activists have been arbitrarily arrested, tortured, and charged with politically motivated offences that include murder, conspiracy and sedition. The Maoists have threatened or attacked activists they believe are linked to the government.

### Jammu and Kashmir

While violence in the northern state of Jammu and Kashmir has been on a decline, security forces responsible for serious rights abuses remain effectively immune from prosecution under the AFSPA.

In September, the state government rejected calls for DNA testing of 2,730 corpses that a police investigative team found in unmarked graves at 38 sites in north Kashmir in July, 2011. Some of the grave-sites are believed to hold victims of enforced disappearance and extrajudicial execution by government security forces dating back to the 1990s.

A number of elected village council leaders resigned in September following threats and attacks from armed separatist militants who oppose any election in Jammu and Kashmir.

### Violence in Assam

In July, violence between indigenous Bodo tribes and Muslim migrant settlers started in Kokrajhar and spread to several districts in Assam, resulting in the deaths of at least 97 people and displacing over 450,000. Authorities in Assam failed to prevent the violence, despite information about increasing tensions between the communities, which have clashed in the past over access to land and resources.

### Freedom of Expression

In 2012, the Centre Government used the Information Technology (Intermediary Guidelines) Rules to tighten internet censorship, raising concerns about restrictions on the right to free speech. Under the rules, intermediaries such as internet service providers and search engines are required to remove content within 36 hours that is deemed offensive. However, criteria for prohibited content are ambiguous and frequently used to stifle criticism of the government.

The government used the colonial-era sedition law without regard for a Supreme Court ruling that sedition requires evidence of incitement. In September, police in Mumbai arrested political cartoonist Aseem Trivedi, acting on a complaint that his cartoons mocked the Indian constitution and the national emblem. He was released after widespread protests. In May, in the southern state of Tamil Nadu, police filed sedition complaints against thousands of people who peacefully protested against the construction of a nuclear power plant. In Orissa and Chhattisgarh states, sedition cases have been filed against activists and lawyers suspected of supporting armed Maoist groups.

The government continued to use the Foreign Contributions Regulation Act (FCRA) to restrict access to foreign assistance by domestic nongovernmental organisations.

## Protection of Children's Rights

Children remained at risk of abuse, with a large number forced into dangerous forms of labour, and without proper access to health-care and education.

India has one of the largest populations of malnourished children in the world. According to government estimates, at least 40 per cent of children are vulnerable to sex trafficking, homelessness, forced labour, drug abuse, and crime—and need protection.

The government took some significant steps in 2012 to improve children's rights. In April, the Supreme Court upheld the government decision to provide universal access to primary education, requiring that private schools reserve 25 per cent of seats for underprivileged children. In May, Parliament passed a new law to protect children from sexual abuse. In August, the government issued a blanket ban on employing children under 14, reversing a former law that only prohibited employment in hazardous jobs.

## Women's Rights

Violence against women and girls continued in 2012, with increased reports of sexual assault, including against even those with disabilities. The government had yet to properly investigate and prosecute sexual abuse in police custody.

In June 2012, Pinki Pramanik, a renowned woman athlete, was arrested on allegations of rape. Male police officers mistreated her while taking her into custody and authorities conducted 'gender determination' tests in violation of her rights to consent, privacy, and dignity. A video of her undergoing some part of the abusive examination was made public.

India has yet to enact amendments to reform its penal laws to recognise a wide range of sexual offences. While the Centre government modified its protocols for handling rape investigations, removing questions on the degrading 'two-finger test,' the changes still fall short of World Health Organisation (WHO) guidelines on sexual assault, especially regarding medical treatment for victims.

India has a strong law to curb child marriages but the government also pursues discriminatory policies. In central India's Madhya Pradesh state, for example, adult candidates are barred from taking state civil service examinations if they were forced to marry as children. The government continued to limit its nutrition programmes for pregnant mothers in many states to women aged 19 and older, and up to two live births only, excluding many young mothers from benefits.

## Abuses in Extractive Industry

A breakdown in government oversight over India's mining sector has led to rampant corruption and, in some cases, to serious harm to health, environments, and livelihoods of mining-affected communities.

In September, the government of the western state of Goa cancelled all mining licences to examine whether proper procedures were followed to mitigate the negative impact on health and environment. The same month, after a year-long suspension, mining activity was allowed to partially resume in the southern Karnataka state, on condition that no environmental restrictions are violated. However, the government failed to enforce protection mechanisms in other parts of the country.

### Access to Palliative Care

The Indian government took several important steps in 2012 to address the suffering of hundreds of thousands of persons with incurable diseases from pain and other symptoms. It has begun to actively encourage regional cancer centres, many of which do not currently offer palliative care, to ensure such services become available. The government is also preparing amendments to the Narcotic Drugs and Psychotropic Substances Act, which, if adopted, would improve the medical availability of morphine. More than seven million people in India require palliative care every year.

### Death Penalty

In November, India hanged Ajmal Kasab, the only surviving Pakistani gunman from the November 2008 Mumbai attacks in which 10 members of the Lashkar-e-Taiba, Pakistan-based terrorist group, killed more than 160 people. It was the first execution in India since 2004, ending an eight-year unofficial *moratorium*.

India maintains that it imposes capital punishment in only the 'rarest of rare' cases. In July, 14 retired judges asked the President to commute the death sentences of 13 inmates erroneously upheld by the Supreme Court over the past nine years. This followed the court's admission that these death sentences were rendered *per incuriam* (out of error or ignorance). In November, the Supreme Court also conceded that the 'rarest of rare' standard has not been applied uniformly over the years and that the principles for judging what constitutes 'rarest of rare' crimes need 'a fresh look.'

### International Role

India's foreign policy in the region continues to be influenced by strategic and economic concerns about China's growing influence in Burma, Nepal, Pakistan and Sri Lanka.

India took some positive steps toward promoting human rights and accountability globally. In March, India voted for a United States-led resolution at the United Nations Human Rights Council (HRC) calling for post-war reconciliation and accountability in Sri Lanka. This marked a significant change of position by India, which has traditionally refrained from publicly criticizing the Sri Lankan government on well-documented war crimes and related abuses.

In February, India voted in favour of a UN Security Council resolution on Syria backing an Arab League plan concerning the escalating violence there. In July, India again voted with Western governments at the Security Council in favour of a resolution on Syria, which if adopted, would have extended the mandate of the United Nations Supervision Mission in Syria (UNSMIS) and threatened sanctions if demands that Syrian authorities end abuses were not met.

## Key International Actors

India has traditionally followed a foreign policy based on the principle of non-interference and deems any criticism on human rights issues as interference in its domestic affairs. As a result, most countries, including the US and the European Union (EU), prefer to discuss these issues with India in private rather than publicly press it to improve its rights record.

However, in May, several UN member-states made significant recommendations during the UN Universal Periodic Review (UPR) of India's human rights record. Recommendations included calls for India to ratify international treaties against torture and enforced disappearance, repeal the death penalty as well as the much-abused AFSPA, and protect the rights of *Dalits,* religious minorities, women, children, and tribal groups. The Indian government has responded by committing to address some of the recommendations, but ignored those that required substantive action against impunity.

India invited the UN special rapporteur on extrajudicial, summary, or arbitrary executions, and the UN special rapporteur on the sale of children, child pornography, and child prostitution to visit the country. After his visit in March, Christof Heyns, the special rapporteur on extrajudicial, summary, or arbitrary executions, expressed concerns over 'high levels of impunity' enjoyed by police and armed forces, recommended that the AFSPA be repealed, and called for establishing a commission of inquiry to investigate extrajudicial killings.

# End Violence Against Women, Children, Minorities

The Indian government's inability to protect women and children from rape and sexual violence undermines its commitment to uphold the rights of all Indians, said. Human Rights Watch During 2013, the authorities also failed to enforce laws that protect vulnerable communities including *Dalits,* religious minorities, and tribal groups. Government efforts to increase mass surveillance raised concerns over rights to privacy and free speech.

"International attention to sexual attacks in India led to a new law, but should have spurred the government towards systemic changes to make real progress on this issue," said Meenakshi Ganguly, South Asia director at Human Rights Watch. "The government has also failed to keep its promises of reforms to create a responsive police force, and to repeal laws that protect the armed forces from prosecution."

In the *World Report 2014,* its 24th edition, Human Rights Watch reviews human rights practices in more than 90 countries. Syria's widespread killings of civilians elicited horror but few steps by world leaders to stop it, Human Rights Watch said. A reinvigorated doctrine of 'responsibility to protect' seems to have prevented some mass atrocities in Africa. Majorities in power in Egypt and other countries have suppressed dissent and minority rights. And Edward Snowden's revelations about US surveillance programmes reverberated around the globe.

India has strong legislation to protect rights, Human Rights Watch said, but entrenched corruption and lack of accountability foster human rights violations. The numerous civil society groups, which play a crucial advocacy role in addressing these problems through protests and free expression, are increasingly at risk due to misused sedition laws and financial regulations.

In April, India rolled out a Central Monitoring System for all phone and Internet communications, which rights groups fear could lead to abuse in the absence of adequate oversight or safeguards for the right to privacy.

The courage and persistence of victims' families and human rights activists did result in court interventions and investigations in several cases of extrajudicial killings in which the security forces had falsely claimed that the deaths occurred during armed exchanges or in self-defence.

In the run-up to the 2014 parliamentary elections, there was an increase in communal clashes between Hindus and Muslims. There is risk of additional violence as political interest groups seek to exploit tensions between the two communities, Human Rights Watch said.

Maoist insurgents in central and eastern India continued to attack civilians and security forces, while villagers remained at risk of arbitrary arrests and torture by state forces. Maoists continued to attack schools and government security forces occupied school buildings for operations in violation of court orders. Internationally, India engaged in efforts to promote human rights in Sri Lanka, Afghanistan, and Burma but did little to address the crises outside of South Asia, such as in Syria.

"India's aspirations to play a more powerful role in world affairs won't be taken seriously so long as it shuns efforts to promote human rights abroad and at home," Ganguly said.

It emerges that we have to go a long way in order to provide human rights to common man. The rights are enshrined in constitutions but in real situation the rights are available only to those who are powerful and have sufficient money in their pocket. Else it has been discussed in the body that the human rights are generally not available to common man in totality. What is available is the deprivatory human rights, discriminatory human rights and differential human rights. We have to go a long mile to achieve the target of restoring human rights of the down trodden section of these societies. The human rights activists and the human rights Watch, they are very active in extending support for preservation and promotion of human rights in the interest of the people for achieving human rights in totality.

I have mentioned in my two books, i.e, *Dynamics of development in tribal India* and *Sustainable development* that the tribals *Dalits* and *Mahadalits* are generally having following three human rights.

(1). Deprivatory Human Rights;
(2). Discriminatory Human Rights; and
(3). Differential Human Rights.

The details of each above Human Rights have been discussed in details in those two books.

# 9

# Human Rights Violations by Police in Custody

It is necessary to define the concept of 'Human Rights Violations in Police Custody'. This concept is known in many ways - 'police brutality', 'police torture', 'police excesses', 'custodial violence' and 'lock-up crimes'.

The general meaning attributed to this concept is that people in police custody are not being treated with the complete dignity and rights, which the citizens in a model democratic state deserve. The practice of causing degradation to the status of an individual, any physical or mental harassment to him, or any deprivation of his personal liberty or fundamental rights of freedom in police custody can be treated as human rights violations in police custody. But ironically, this is considered as necessary for law enforcement by police.

**Pic. 9.1**

Though, India is playing a vital role in the United Nation's system and other world forums for the protection of human rights, the recent Supreme Court decisions reveal that the human rights of the persons in the custody of police continue to be violated, unabated even today. Most of the reports on human rights violations in police custody show that they have emanated from indigenous sources. Main focus of these reports is on torture, including rape and deaths in custody. The reports criticise practices that are blatantly unconstitutional. The country faces an embarrassing situation, because human rights abuses have become common and a sense of hopelessness intruded our thought and reaction. Justice Krishna Iayer describes our human rights record as 'teasing illusion and promise of unreality'. As far as the protections of human rights of persons in police custody are concerned, the condition in India is not at all satisfactory. There is persistent increase of human rights violations in police custody including rape, custodial violence and death in India. Very often, the suspects and witnesses are picked up in custody illegally by the police and tortured for a long time even without recording it in the general diary. They are tortured for the purpose of extracting confessions, or for recovery of case property, or for securing information about the commission of the crimes irrespective of whether a crime has actually been committed or not. Usually, they are not produced before the magistrate within 24 hours of their arrest. Thus, the worst violations of human rights of person occur during the course of investigation and interrogation when the police resort to third degree methods on the person in custody.

**Pic. 9.2**

In his report to the United Nations Commission on Human Rights in April 2001, the Special Rapporteur on Torture, Sir Nigel Rodley made the following observations about the situation of torture in India:

> While the size and diversity of the country make it difficult to characterise the intensity of the problems all over, it certainly appears that there is a tradition of police brutality and arbitrariness in much of the country, the degree of brutality frequently being sufficiently unrestrained to amount to torture, often with fatal consequences. The brutality is sometimes linked with corruption and extortion and is often deployed in the service of local vested interests, be they economic or official. The use of excessive and indeed unprovoked and unjustified force is common, especially in response to protests demanding rights. The *persecution* of those pursuing complaints against the police is a not infrequent phenomenon... In general, while not absolute,

> the level of impunity among police and security forces seems sufficiently substantial as to conduce a general sense among such officials that their excesses, especially those committed in the line of duty, will at least be tolerated, if not encouraged.

India has a record of flagrant violations of rights at every level. It is really unfortunate that, State, supposed to be the guardian and promoter of human rights, becomes the prime violator. Both the Centre and State Governments are still being condemned by the human rights activists and civil liberty organisations for their negligent attitude towards safeguarding the fundamental freedoms and human dignity. But undermining all these efforts, human rights violations are increasing day by day and life and liberty of the citizens are still being jeopardised by mounting incidents of State violence. Police in our context has a long history of law-breaking. Its record of too little regard for human rights is not a thing of the past; it is flourishing now as ever before.

The Mauryan states were autocratic police states and their functions were political, economic, social and at times religious, and it affected almost all the aspects of human life and allegedly infringed on the privacy of man from the time of conception to cremation.

In the *Arthashastra,* Chanakya mentioned espionage for collecting intelligence and torture for obtaining confessions. But being aware that even innocent persons may also be forced to confess under threat or use of torture, he insisted on corroborative evidence. He also prescribed mutilation of various parts of the body for various offences; chopping of fingers, hands, arms, legs and even blinding. Incidentally, shaving of the head, something our police occasionally do even today to *goondas* is also prescribed in the *Arthashastra.*

From the works of Kalidasa, it appears that the administration of urban police department was not always satisfactory and the integrity of officials was questionable. They were experts in accepting bribes and many of them were alcohol addicts. Watchmen usually wandered about the town either on their routine rounds or in search of thieves. They kept watch on roads and highways with truncheons *(Danda)* in their hands. Even ladies of suspicious activities were seized by them while on duty. Kalidasa records the existence of a band of frontier guards who often oppressed simple and innocent travellers. Persons with suspicious movements were occasionally menaced with torture by policemen. The police exhibited enormous cruelty to extort confession which sometimes proved fatal.

Police under the Islamic and British Rule with the invasion of India by Muslims created new situation wherein the Muslim rulers or *Sultans* followed a policy of discrimination against the Hindus. So, the significance of Muslim rule in India was counterproductive to harmony, justice and equality. The performance of magisterial function by the police *Kotwal* was an important feature, which was also later followed by the English East India Company. When the Emperor or the *Subedar* was not in residence, the capital was ruled by the *Kotwal.* All petty criminal cases were disposed of by him by a summary procedure. He had been vested with power to inflict torture. The Mughal being essentially an urban people, neglected the protection of villages.

The police officials started exploiting the situation to their advantage and became notoriously corrupt and oppressive. They used this opportunity for their personal aggrandisement, mutual revenue, or public plunder. When the English East India Company assumed political responsibilities, there was no stability or peace in the country. Even in the presidency cities of Calcutta, Bombay and Madras, where Europeans were settled in considerable numbers, the police were very inefficient, and the dissatisfaction of the residents was frequently expressed. Extortion and oppression was practised by all ranks of police officials. The administration of police was hopelessly disorganised, mischievously corrupt and utterly inefficient. During the company period, the combination of revenue, judicial and magisterial functions in one person resulted in tyranny; the collection of revenue was made through torture. The complaints became so numerous that on September 9, 1854, the Governor in council of fort St. George appointed a Commission for the investigation of alleged cases of torture at Madras. Charges were made in the British parliament that revenue was being systematically raised with the use of torture by the native officers (*Tahsildars*). Fortunately in 1855, the Torture Commission was appointed to enquire into these complaints. During the period of 1861–1902, the British Government did not pay serious attention to the welfare of the police personnel, especially in the subordinate rank. As a result of low emoluments and absence of welfare amenities, they resorted to corrupt practices and misused their powers. The police force was ill equipped and had acquired a bad name. In order to remove these defects and to reform the policies in regard to personnel administration, a thorough probe became necessary. Therefore, when the Indian Evidence Act was drafted, they included sections 25 and 26 and made the police untrustworthy. Confessions to police or in their presence were made inadmissible in evidence in courts. In a way, these two sections in the Evidence Act, 1872 made the police to use more and more torture on the suspects to elicit confessions and to make a recovery under section 27 of the Indian Evidence Act, 1872. The same Act is in use even today in India.

The British authorities became aware of the police atrocities and later on replaced the system by *Darogas* who were under no proper supervision. They also proved ineffective. The *Darogas* were ultimately replaced by the Magistrates who were not interested in the village affairs in any way nor did they listen to the common grievances of the rural population and consequently did nothing to remove the difficulties of the villagers. The Torture Commission was of the opinion that the main object of the British rulers was to collect revenue with the police help. The police was merely an instrument in the hands of the district officers to enforce the autocratic will of the officers. Later on, the administrative system was changed with one officer for each unit of administration who was approached by the people with all sorts of grievances. Thereupon a collector magistrate was taken as the sole administrator of the district who was authorised to control all the administrative affairs including the police. The police was concerned to maintain law and order not for the good of the people or in public interest but to facilitate collection of revenues and keep the villagers under subjugation. The superintendent of police was made subordinate to the district magistrate with the result that voices were raised against the dual system in the district. This discontentment against the revenue officers and the police officers continued for a pretty long time without much change more or less on the usual patterns.

The British bequeathed a concept of the rule of police. The people at large were put to almost inhuman atrocities and hardships at the hands of local administration principally through the agency of the British police. Police continued to be an object of terror and abhorrence to the general public. The repression carried out during the Indian political movement for independence, mainly through the agency of the police further tainted the already tarnished image of the police in the public mind. In India, the police became a monster machine with tentacles spreading in all the spheres of social and non-social, political and non-political work of the State. During the period from 1914 to 1946, some hurried increase in the Force was sanctioned. Fractional Idealisation of the superior police service had started, but still over 90 percent of the officers were not of Indian origin. During this period there was no substantial improvement in prevention and detection of crime, and rendering satisfactory criminal justice to the people, for entire resources and energies of the police were channelized to safeguard the British Imperial interest in India in the last bid to perpetuate their regime. All sorts of atrocities, which the institution of *Darogahs* had committed on the people in the past were allowed to be committed in innumerable places by the Europeans as well as native police officials in order to suppress the national uprising for freedom of India. In these nefarious acts, the British Government not only incited the police, but also actuated them to behave in this atrocious fashion for ensuring its own safety, stability and consolidation of regime in this sub-continent.

During the period of Indian independence struggle, the police force was considered a terror and was abhorrent to the people. During this periods the repressive attitude of the British Imperialism was adopted through the police agency to crush serious political movements. This was to some extent natural that the loyalty of the police to the Government of that time was unimpeachable due to restrictive regulations and disciplined organisation. Pandit Jawaharlal Nehru has given a graphic description of what happened to him when he demonstrated against the Simon Commission at Lucknow.

> I felt pain all over my body and great fatigue. Almost every part of me seemed to ache; and I was covered with confused wounds and marks of lathis. But, fortunately, I was not injured in any vital spot. Govind Ballabh Pant, who stood by me, offered a much bigger target, being six feet tall; and the injuries he received then have resulted in a painful and persistent malady which prevented him for a long time from straightening his back or leading an active life.

The police had clashed not only with hosts of Congressmen and other patriots actively participating in non-violent anti-government activities; they also attacked innocent people who had no role in the struggle for freedom movement.

## Independence and after

The police culture that existed in the pre-independence period was allowed to continue even after India became independent. The Police Act of 1861 instituted the system of police which is still in force in India. There was no sincere or wholehearted attempt on the part of the governments to redefine the role and responsibilities of the police until the National Police Commission was appointed in 1977. Thus, the police sub-culture that was in existence during the British regime continued to operate and in that culture torture of citizens and calling of bad names against them were permitted and tolerated by the authorities and the general public alike. The police force was not conceived as a service organisation. It was designed as a force to be used against the community but at the same time, it was so constituted and controlled as not to overwhelm its creators. The British used the police to mercilessly violate all human rights and as a result, all police commissions hitherto appointed in India to study the police functioning have been unanimous in their views that the police in India have shown no regard to human rights. Almost all the state commissions have commented adversely on police behavior. The conclusion part of Punjab Police Commission reads:

> The Commission is of the opinion that most of the investigating officers have no training in the use of scientific methods of investigation, and the only method of investigation known to them is that of third degree. Third degree methods are used by them in one fun or the other to extract confessions or else such statements as make the use of section 27 of the Indian Evidence Act possible. The Central Investigation Agency, a special branch of this organisation charged with the duty of investigation (of) heinous crime, has acquired notoriety in the public for third degree methods and is styled as the *'butcher-khana'*. Instances of people dying as a result of torture by the police are not wanting and this is a big blot on organisation.

Before the Maharashtra Police Commission a number of witnesses stated that the police use third degree methods and policemen, particularly in the lower ranks, are often rude and discourteous to the public, and that the police force is an instrument of oppression. The Tamil Nadu Police Commission further found that "when a person goes to a police station with a complaint no one listens to him willingly or patiently", and if the complainant insists on being heard immediately he receives a shower of abuses in 'vile language' and is 'threatened with some sort of action against himself.' The Delhi Police Commission also stated: "Indeed, almost all the public witnesses who appeared before the Commission, have testified that the police have no public image at all. People do not trust them because they are unreliable and corrupt. People do not love them because they are vindictive and cruel".The third all India Police Commission in its *Fourth Report* discussed the use of third degree methods in the investigation of offences. It expressed regret that several police officers "under pressure of work and driven by a desire to achieve quick results", use force on witnesses, suspects and accused. The Commission voiced concern at the inclination of some of the supervisory ranks to countenance this practice in a bid to achieve quick results by short-cut methods.

**Pic. 9.3**

Police brutality and torture during the last three decades show that the custodians of law have become lawbreakers. The *lathi*-wielding attitude, the brutal abuse, its brutality of power and the use of third degree methods by the police have become the order of the day. After the horrid experience of police brutality during emergency, police oppressions at present in many states have become very common. Major techniques of physical torture adopted by the police were stamping on the bare body with heeled boots, beating with cane on the bare soles of feet, beating on the spine, beating with rifle butt, inserting live electric wires into the crevices of the body, burning with lighted cigarettes and candle flames, rubbing of chilli powder in the nose and rectum.

*Emergency Period*

There is an inevitable link between state of emergency and grave violations of human rights. Article 4(2) of the International

Covenant on Civil and Political Rights lays down that people should enjoy their human rights even during the time of emergency. Right to life, immunity from inhuman or cruel treatment, equality before law, freedom of thought, etc. should have to be protected by the police even during the period of emergency. Indian Constitution, under Article 359, provides that the right to life and liberty under Article 21 should not be suspended even when the rights under part III of the Constitution are suspended during the period of emergency. This means that the Constitution preserves some basic rights of life and liberty even during emergency and the police are to enforce them. The right to life includes freedom from torture, police excesses, inhuman treatment, arbitrary arrest, etc. But in India during the internal emergency the highest authority in the land became the worst violator of democratic norms and the lawlessness of the police knew no bounds.

### The First Emergency and its Continuance

On October 26th, 1962, an Emergency was declared under Article 352 in view of the sudden conflict with China in the Himalayan border regions. A few days later by presidential order the enforcement in any court of fundamental rights guaranteed by the Constitution under Article 14, 19, 21 and 22 was also suspended.

Though, hostilities with China came to an end with the ceasefire declared on November 21st, 1962, the proclamation of emergency continued, fundamental rights under Article 19, remained suspended, and right to enforce in any court the fundamental rights guaranteed by was also remained suspended.

### The Second Emergency and its Prolongation

Following the second proclamation of Emergency, all the rights to freedoms guaranteed by Article 19, stood automatically suspended. Parliament then passed in quick succession the Maintenance of Internal Security Act and the Defence of India Act, and the Centre Government promulgated the Defence of India Rules, 1971. A rigid and unprecedented press censorship was imposed – there was a complete ban on reports of speeches in Parliament and of reports of all cases in courts other than the names of counsel and judge and the operative part of the decision. The President's satisfaction about the need to declare an emergence was declared by Constitutional Amendment to be not only final and conclusive, but also non-justiceable. By a Presidential ordinance amending MISA, the statutory requirement of the detainee's right to be informed of the grounds of arrest was deleted–it was sufficient for the authorities to declare that the arrest was made to 'safeguard the security of India'. Widest powers of detention were thus vested in the Centre Government and the State Government–which meant any person authorised to act for the Centre Government or the State Government: theoretically, even a desk clerk! And the power to detain was not confined only to those in the secretariats in Delhi or the state capitals; it could also be exercised by every district magistrate and every commissioner of police in every town and village in every state.

The almost 19 months of National Emergency imposed by Indira Gandhi between 1975 and 1977 have been seen by many analysts as the turning point in the post-colonial history of India.

During emergency as many as 6,851 detention of leaders of opposition parties were made under preventive detention laws.

It was also the time of the crumbling of the police order. Emergency made the hierarchy *topsy-turvy.* The politicians encouraged subversion of the chain of command. The corrective mechanism available in the police force was neutralised. Torture and mayhem could not be effectively controlled. The current methodology of third degree does not show any remarkable refinement over the methods described by the Torture Commission.

The methods of torture were described by the Torture Commission: Among the principal tortures in vogue in police cases we find the following: twisting a rope tightly round the entire ankle or leg so as to impede circulation; lifting up by the moustache; suspending by arms while tied behind the back; *searing* with hot irons; placing scratching insects, such as the carpenter beetle, on the navel, *scrotum* and other sensitive parts; dipping in wells and rivers, till the party is half suffocated; squeezing the testicles; beating with sticks; prevention of sleep; nipping the flesh with pincers; putting pepper or red chillies in the eyes or introducing them into the private parts of men or women; these cruelties occasionally persevered until death sooner or later ensues.

Emergency distorted police functioning considerably in Kerala as in most other states. Senior police officers were as much responsible for this as the politicians in power. Whereas a number of excesses did not receive any attention whatsoever, one case which shook the polity of Kerala once emergency was lifted in

1977, was the infamous Rajan case, where a student was tortured to death in a remote police camp, an act so brutal in nature that the entire populace of Kerala revolted in no uncertain measure. During this period, various types of police atrocities were committed upon the poorer people, students, teenagers and teachers. A retired professor whose son was tortured to death by police, describes his feelings on hearing the experience of the victims in the Kakkayam police camp: Koru, Benhar and Chathamangalam Rajan told me about Kakkayam camp, shivering while narrating stories of blood clotting torture, as if trying hard to forget. When the victims of police torture showed me the never fading scars of torture on their bodies, saliva filled my mouth and darkness, my eyes. A whistle echoed in my ears.

The professor describes the atmosphere in the camp: Mr J would sit on a chair and pass orders while police jeeps rushed in and out and youngsters were dragged forth. They were beaten, and then tied to a wooden bench with their hands and legs down. A heavy wooden roller would be rolled over their thighs; many could not stand the pain, and fell unconscious. To prevent them from crying out, the police pushed cloth into their mouths. Afterwards, they would be brought before Mr J. While questioning them, he would roll a sharpened pencil in his hands; suddenly he would stab the pencil in the muscles worked loose from the bones on the thighs of the torture. Koru said that at that moment you thought it would be better to die. The cries from being stabbed with that pencil could be heard outside the camp. He depicts the plight of his son in the camp:

My son Rajan was tortured first. They asked him where the rifle was that had been stolen during the attack on the Kayanna police station. He had never been beaten even once in his short life, so with the first round of torture he became weary. Then he was tied to the wooden bench and rolled. He cried out for his mother; they stuffed cloth into his mouth. At the end of the torture, to get away from it he told them that he would find the rifle. Then he was taken to Mr J., who told the policemen to take Rajan to a jeep and go in search of the rifle. Then he cried again. He told them that he was not aware of the rifle at all, and had said that to escape further torture. Mr P. began kicking him in his stomach with his heavy police boots. With a loud cry he fell back and writhed on the floor, then became quiet and motionless... They packed Rajan's body into a sack and took it away in a jeep. They burned it in the midst of some forest with sugar, to ensure that not even the bones would be left behind.

## During the Janata Regime

Even after the defeat of Mrs Gandhi at the polls in 1977 and the coming to power of a broad coalition, for almost two years there was a relatively low profile of the range and extent of civil rights activities. In the early days of its rule, the Janata Party took limited steps to restore the democratic rights of the people. But then came the halt. There was an attempt by the Janata government even to perpetuate preventive detention, despite the electoral pledge that Maintenance of Internal Security Act would be repealed. No doubt this law was repealed at the centre, but it remained prevailed very much in the states.

## In the Eighties

The alleged methods of torture in this period include hanging people upside down, severe beating (sometimes until the victims limbs are broken), burning and plying heavy rollers on the victims leg. In some cases, the use of electric shocks has been reported. Such methods were particularly common during the investigation of ordinary criminal offences such as theft, and are most widely used against the poorer sections of Indian society, notably the *adivasis,* tribal and *harijans.* In the early 1981, the Indian press reported detailed account of people suspected of ordinary criminal offences whose legs had been broken and then twisted by the police in Varanasi and Gazipur in Utter Pradesh. Cases of torture and death in custody are widely reported in press, and in a number of instances, have been investigated by civil liberties organisations. When magisterial inquiries found that deaths in custody were due to police brutality the only punishment the guilty officials was given is that they were only suspended from duty or transferred. Sometimes police officials were later on reinstated.

## After Eighties

After 1980, police has resorted to more repressive techniques as not to leave any scar of police atrocities on the body of victims. Even minors were not spared at the hands of police. A newspaper published a report, according to which, young boys of 10 to 14 years were being supplied to detainees for their delectation and a boy name Munna was in agony because after the way he was used he was unable to sit. The helpless boy gives the description of police torture in a telling manner: I was taken to Baz Mandi police station and beaten up. My feet were swollen. Then they put a bandage around my forehead and passed electric shocks through it.

After the late eighties the incidents of death through torture in police custody has been on the increase. In the 1980s and 1990s. hundreds of people were tortured, extrajudicially executed, or disappeared. Despite calls by human rights organisations including Amnesty International for impartial investigations into these human rights violations, there has still been no comprehensive investigation into the pattern of human rights violations perpetrated by police. Amnesty International believes that this situation has facilitated the continuation of torture and other illegal activities by police. Methods of torture used in the past against political detainees by police including rolling wooden rollers over the legs of suspects thereby tearing muscles, stretching the legs apart and electric shock treatment–are now used against common criminal suspects or against individuals detained merely for the purpose of extortion.

Police have established several centres where inhuman and sadistic tortures are inflicted. Corruption has been rampant and the interrogation officers have been extorting money for the release of innocent persons. The persons killed due to torture were said to be disposed of in clandestine manner and most of them were thrown in the waterways or fields. These arrests were made by police without FIR and therefore, treated as deaths due to mutual rivalry of militant groups. In other cases, no doubt, FIR is registered but a concocted story is made that in course of recovery of arms, when detainee was being carried by the police party, he ran away or killed by militants when they tried to liberate him.

The police were faced with a peculiar problem in Punjab during the days of militancy. Police were killing people by the thousands, many of them innocents. In the state of Punjab and Haryana torture has been institutionalised in the form of group of policemen who excel in method of Interrogation called criminal interrogation agency headed by an official of Inspector rank. The 'cause of arrest' is not on the record and if the victim dies during interrogation the agency denies ever having seen him. If he confesses or helps the interrogators recovering anything connected with the crime, he is transferred to a proper police station and a case is registered against him. If he refuses to confess or looks innocent after inflicting torture, he is just let off, often at night, and told to be wise enough not to complain to anyone. People never complain to anyone due to fear of police torture.

The police was using several brutal methods to get forced confessions from innocent people. This inhuman torture starts with a thorough beating of the victim. And, if the victim refused to confess, he was taken outside where the victims is stripped and then made to sit on the top of a sharp bamboo. After this, the police men start pressing hard on the victims shoulders in order to impale him. The torture is enough to make any victim admit to any crime. The police has destroyed the life of several people by using such third degree methods.

Another method of torture adopted by police in Madhya Pradesh was *Laxman Jhula*. This barbaric form of torture is used to terrorise the persons either to extract money or to get confession. The victim in stripped of all his cloths, and then hung upside down from the ring fixed in the roof of the room with the help of rope. The hands of the victim are tied. Then they start thrashing of the victim on the sole of his feet–such a place of beating is used because it leaves no marks. If the victim is still reluctant to confess the torture is carried to a still vicious stage, the line wires are place against victim's I genitals and electric shocks are repeatedly administered till the victim is helpless with pain. The torture leads to impotence. Various laws have been passed by the Union Government and the State Governments enabling the Government to detain any person so as to prevent him acting against the security or defence of the country.

The Constitution (Fifty-ninth) Amendment Act, 1988, which was passed by Parliament and assented to by the President, raised serious implications not only for Punjab but also for the future of democracy in India. The introduction of Article 359-A seeking to amend Article 352 in relation to Punjab by providing that an emergency could be declared for an additional reason, namely, when 'the integrity of India is threatened by internal disturbance in the whole or any part of the territory of Punjab' was considered denial of right to life in Punjab. The obvious object of the amendment was considered to bring the people of Punjab under emergency regulations forthwith. Article 358 was amended and the government acquired the right to suspend Article 19 including the right to life. Much worse was the amendment in Article 359 which enabled the government to suspend the Article as and when proclamation of emergency is made in respect of Punjab or in any part of its territory. The total effect of the suspension of this Article could be, that a person can be deprived of his life and liberty without any sanction of law; he could be harassed, detained, tortured and even killed, and he or his family members would have no right to approach the court for relief.

According to human right activist like Rajeev Dhavan the existing laws and Act, Preventive Detention Act, Unlawful Association Act and the provisions in Indian Penal Code are sufficient to deal with terrorism. The analysis shows that number of illegal detentions, police tortures and custodial deaths are rising day by day. Though, the judiciary has been keen to award compensation in such cases, the criminal procedure code is silent on the issue. So, it is recommended that some specific provisions to ensure compensation to the persons illegally detained and to the members of the family of a person died in police custody should be included in the code.

# 10
# Violation of Woman Rights

## Violation of Right to Equality and Right to Protection against Gender Discrimination

Discrimination against the girl child starts the moment she enters into the mother's womb. The child is exposed to gender differences since birth and in recent times even before birth, in the form of sex–determination tests leading to feticide and female infanticide. The home, which is supposed to be the most secured place, is where women are most exposed to violence. If a girl child opens her eyes in any way, she is killed after her birth by different cruel methods in some parts of the country. Thus, the very important right to life is denied to women. In India, men are always assumed to be superior to women and are given more preference. The World Human Rights Conference in Vienna first recognised gender–based violence as a human rights violation in 1993. The same was declared by United Nations Declaration in 1993.

### Violation of Right to Education

Education is considered as means of development of personality and awareness. Education is one of the most important human rights but the position of women's education in India is not at all satisfactory. Young girls may be brought up to believe that they are suited only to certain professions or in some cases to serve as wives and mothers.

Despite in the improvement in the literacy rate after independence, there continues to be large gap between the literacy levels of men and women. Almost half the women populations are even unable to recognise language characters. At least 60 million girls lack access to primary education in India. Due to large percentage of uneducated women in India, they are not even aware of their basic human rights and can never fight for them.

## Violation of Political Right

The political status of women in India is very unsatisfactory, particularly their representation in higher political institutions Parliament and provincial bodies of legislation, which hampers their effective role in influencing the government initiatives and policies regarding women's welfare and development. Their representation has been unable to reach even 10 per cent in Lok Sabha. Thus, it is clear that: (a) there is male domination in Indian politics and almost all the parties give very little support to women in election despite their vocal support for 33 per cent reservation of seats for women in Parliament and Provincial Legislative. Bodies, and (b) women have made initiatives in political participation but they have not been accepted in politics.

## Violation of Right to Property

In most of the Indian families, women do not own property in their own names and do not get share of parental property. Due to weak enforcement of laws protecting them, women continue to have little access to land and property. In fact, some of the laws discriminate against women, when it comes to land and property rights. Though, women have been given rights to inheritance, but the sons had an independent share in the ancestral property, while the daughter's shares were based on the share received by the father. Hence, father could anytime disinherit daughter by renouncing his share but the son will continue to have a share in his own right. The married daughters facing harassment have no rights in ancestral home.

## Violation of Right to Protection of Health

According to the *World Bank report,* malnutrition is the major cause of female infertility. The presence of excessive malnutrition among female children as compared to male children is basically due to differences in the intra–family allocation of food between the male and female children. Normally, the male members are fed before the female members of the family. According to *Human Development Report,* in rural Punjab, 21 per cent of girls in low income families suffer from severe malnutrition as compared with three per cent of boys in the same family. Even the low income boys are far better than upper income girls. Girl babies are fewer breast–fed than boy babies. 60 per cent of girl babies are born with low birth weight. Sometimes due to economic distress and natural calamities like floods, droughts, or earthquakes, the discrimination against the female child increases. Moreover, it has been confirmed by various studies that the girl's diet is inferior to the boy's diet both in quality and quantity. Boys are given more nutritive foods like milk, eggs, butter, ghee, fruits, and vegetables as compared to girls. Due to this inferior quality diet, girls are more vulnerable to infections and diseases. The reason again is that families spend less on medication for girls than for boys.

## Violation of Right to Equal Oppertunity for Employment and Right to Get Equal Wages for Equal Work

The employment of the women in agriculture, traditional industries and in sizeable section of new industries is declining at a very fast rate. The reason is that the adoption of new technological changes requires new skill, knowledge and training. And women in India, who constitute a large share of world's illiterate lack such skills and knowledge. The studies have also showed that for the same task, women are paid less than the males. Technological changes in agriculture and industry are throwing out women from the production process. The women workers are concentrated only for certain jobs which require so–called female skills. Thus, Indian labour market is adverse to women workers. It shows that, the role of women in large scale industries and technology based businesses is very limited. But even in the small-scale industries their participation is very low. Only 10.11 per cent of the micro and small enterprises are owned by women today. Statistics show that only 15 per cent of the senior management posts are held by the women. In agriculture where women comprise of the majority of agricultural labourers, the average wage of women on an average is 30–50 per cent less than that of men.

## Violation of Right to Live with Dignity Eve Teasing and Sexual Abuse

Eve-teasing is an act of terror that violates a woman's body, space and self–respect. It is one of the many ways through which a woman is systematically made to feel inferior, weak and afraid.

Whether it is an obscene word whispered into a woman's ear; offensive remarks on her appearance; any intrusive way of touching any part of women's body; a gesture which is perceived and intended to be vulgar: all these acts represent a violation of woman's person and her bodily integrity. Thus, eve-teasing denies a woman's fundamental right to move freely and carry herself with dignity, solely on the basis of her sex. There is no particular places where eve–teasers congregate. No place is really 'safe' for women. Roads, buses, train, cinema halls, parks, beaches, even a woman's house and neighbourhood may be sites where her self – worth is abused.

## Violation of Right from Society, State and Family System

### (1). Child Marriage

Child marriage has been traditionally prevalent in India and continues to this date. Discrimination against the girl begins even before their birth and continues as they grow. According to the law, a girl cannot be married until she has reached the age of 18 at least. But the girl in India is taken as a burden on the family. Sometimes the marriages are settled even before the birth of the child. In south India, marriages between cousins are common as they believe that a girl is secured as she has been married within the clan. Parents also believe that it is easy for the child–bride to adapt to new environment as well as it is easy for others to mould the child to suit their family environment. Some believe that they marry girls at an early age so as to avoid the risk of their unmarried daughters getting pregnant. This shows that the reasons for child marriages in India are so baseless. Basically, this phenomenon of child marriage is linked to poverty, illiteracy, dowry, landlessness and other social evils.

The impact of child marriage is widowhood, inadequate socialisation, education deprivation, lack of independence to select the life partner, lack of economic independence, low health/nutritional levels as a result of early/frequent pregnancies in an unprepared psychological state of young bride. However, the Indian boys have to suffer less due to male dominated society. Around 40 per cent child marriages occur in India. A study conducted by 'Family Planning Foundation' showed that the mortality rates were higher among babies born to women under 18. Another study showed that around 56 per cent girls from poorer families were married underage and became mothers.

So, all this indicate that immediate steps should be taken to stop the evil of child marriage.

### (2). Dowry Harassment and Bride Burning

The demand of dowry by the husband and his family and then killing of the bride because of not bringing enough dowry to the in – laws has become a very common crime these days. In spite of the Dowry Prohibition Act passed by the government, which has made dowry demands in wedding illegal, the dowry incidents are increasing day by day. According to survey, around 5,000 women die each year due to dowry deaths and at least a dozen die each day in 'kitchen fires'.

### (3). Rape

Young girls in India often are the victims of rape. Almost 255 of rapes are of girls under 16 years of age. The law against rape is unchanged from 120 years. In rape cases, it is very torturing that the victim has to prove that she has been raped. The victim finds it difficult to undergo medical examination immediately after the trauma of assault. Besides this, the family 'too' is reluctant to bring in prosecution due to family prestige and hard police procedures.

### (4). Domestic Violence

Wife beating, abuse by alcoholic husbands are the violence done against women which are never publicly acknowledged. The cause is mainly the man demanding the hard earned money of the wife for his drinking. But an Indian woman always tries to conceal it as they are ashamed of talking about it. Interference of in–laws and extra marital affairs of the husbands are the another cause of such violence. The pity women are unwilling to go to court because of lack of alternative support system.

Thus, all these violence done against women raise the question mark that how these special rights being given to women are helping them? What are the benefits of framing such laws for the women? Are they really helping them? Will the women really be given an equal status to men one day? All these questions are still unanswered. There is still long way to go to answer such questions.

## References

1. *Crimes in India–2010,* NCRB, Ministry of Home Affairs.
2. Jalbert. E. Susanne.,2000 *Women Entrepreneurs in the Global Economy,* March 17, 2000
3. Shashi, Krishan July 1, 2008 Indian Democracy and Women's Human Rights *Madhya Pradesh Journal of Social Sciences.*
4. United Nations Department of public Information DPI/1772/ HR – February 1996.
5. Poonam Dhanda 2012 *Status of Women in India* RBSA Publications.
6. Madhurima 2010 Readings in Sociology New Academic Publishing Co.

# 11

# Human Rights Violations in Administration in India

## Constitutional Mandate

Justice, social, economic and political is the constitutional aim proclaimed in the preamble of The Constitution of India which contains the requisite guidelines and provides for the infrastructure for attaining it. The fundamental rights guaranteed under the Constitution include prohibition of traffic in human beings and forced labour (Article 23), freedom of conscience and free profession, practice and propagation of religion (Article 25), protection of interests of minorities including their right to establish and administer educational institutions (Article 29 and 30), right to protection of life and personal liberty (Article 21), protection against arrest and detention (Article 22), and right to Constitutional remedies (Article 32). Anyone acquainted with the silent zeal with which the Indian courts have safeguarded the rights of the people as reflected in the judicial pronouncements will instantly know that the instances of human rights violations that are bound to occur in any social order due to conflicting interests of its components are mere aberrations that get corrected by the sound constitutional mechanism of this vibrant democracy.

## The International Efforts

Human rights violations occur through human beings and human agencies and constitute typical social aberrations. The mechanism of judicial justice is devised in all civilised societies to remedy the wrongs that may be perpetrated through individual, executive, legislative injustices or even injustices caused by judicial system itself. In an orderly society a check on the indiscriminate individual or collective behaviour is essential to prevent breakdown and anarchy. If rule of law is to prevail regulation of conduct, violation of human rights becomes an essential aspect of governance of the country. The right to access to justice as contained in the relevant international human rights instruments forms an important basis for strengthening the rule of law through the administration of justice. The importance of ensuring respect for the rule of law and human rights in the administration of justice, particularly in post-conflict situations as a crucial contribution to building peace and justice and ending impunity can hardly be over emphasised. The office of the High Commissioner for Human Rights has done commendable work on development of human rights which includes organising various activities aimed at enhancing the promotion and protection of human rights in the field of administration of justice within the framework of the United Nations Decade for Human Rights Education, 1995-2004. In the Resolution adopted by the General Assembly in the fifty-fifth session on Agenda item 60 (b), it was resolved to strengthen the capacity of all the member countries to implement the principles and practices of democracy and respect for human rights, including minority rights and "to eliminate the increasing acts of racism and xenophobia in many societies and to promote greater harmony and tolerance in all societies." No effort should be spared domestically or internationally to ensure that all civilian populations that suffer disproportionately the consequences of mob violence, natural disaster and other humanitarian emergencies are rendered every assistance and protection so that they can resume normal life as soon as possible. Judicial institutions have a major role to play in this direction.

## The Approach of Municipal Courts

By Article 51 of The Constitution of India the state is enjoined with a duty *inter alia* to promote international peace and security, maintain just and honourable relations, and foster respect for international law and treaty obligations in dealings of organised peoples, with one another. In the absence of contrary legislation, municipal courts in India are under an obligation, within legitimate limits, to so interpret the municipal statute as to avoid confrontation with the comity of nations, or the well-established principles of International Law as held by the Supreme Court (see *Gramophone Co. Vs. Birendra AIR 1984 SC 667* ). The provisions of International conventions/covenants which elucidate and effectuate the fundamental rights guaranteed by The Constitution of India, can be relied upon by courts in India as facets of those fundamental rights and would therefore be enforceable (see People's Union for Civil Liberties V. Union of India, *(1997) 3 SCC 433)*. The Supreme Court and the High Courts in India are obliged to apply international instruments and conventions when there is no inconsistency between them and the corresponding domestic laws, (see *Apparel Export Promotion Council VAK Chopra (1999) 1 SCC 759*). If two constructions of the municipal law are possible, the courts should lean in favour of adopting such construction as would harmonies provisions of the municipal law with the international law or treaty obligations (see *ADM V, Shivkant Shukla (1976) 2 SCC 521)*

## The Ambit of Judicial Power

The judicial power and independence that the Indian judiciary enjoys is enviable even in many democratic and developed countries. It is an understanding of highest cultural order that permits judiciary to play its role fearlessly and respect its verdicts in legislative and executive spheres. Laws inconsistent with or in derogation of the fundamental rights are void to the extent of inconsistency and the state is ordained not to make any law which takes away or abridges the fundamental rights, and any law made in contravention of this provision shall to the extent of contravention be void (Article 13 of The Constitution of India). The Constitution of India expressly confers upon the courts the power of judicial review. To specifically safeguard the fundamental rights, the courts are assigned a special role by this provision and are required to determine finally the constitutionality of an impugned statute. The superior courts have high prerogative power to issue commands to the executive in cases of failure of statutory duty by the executive. The subordinate courts in a state are kept under the control jurisdiction of the high court of that state to ensure separation of judiciary and its independence from the executive. Once the court is satisfied as to the public mischief to be remedied, it would not insist on the *locus standi* of the petitioners, who may not have any personal interest in the matter.

## Internal and External Obstructions

There are three outstanding forms of social control, i.e. the control of the behaviour of individuals through some sort of pressure and these are: organised religion which can exert pressure by religious teaching and appeal to a religious sense; public opinion or morality which can exert pressure through organisations; and the administration of justice by the state by enforcing the accepted norms of behaviour for orderly conduct and peace. With an easy access to the wide jurisdiction of the superior courts and an elaborate system of legal aid to the poor, one would think that the genuine grievances resulting from the violations of the fundamental rights should be redressed without any obstacles. There have, however, been both internal and external obstructions that tend to prevent justice from reaching where needed most in certain delicate areas of human relationship.

## The Quality of Manpower

Amongst the biggest obstacles to justice is the unseen obstacle of the mindset of the dispensers of justice. Without a revolution of the spirit, the forces which produced the iniquities of the old order continue to be operative, posing a constant threat to the process of reform and regeneration. Judges, at times, function under severe pressure and time constraints. They must, therefore, be persons equipped with adequate knowledge, understanding and have competence required to resolve complex issues without prejudice. It is difficult to detect when gender bias, religious bias and even racial bias find their way into judicial acts. When the Judge lacks a proper understanding of law to deal with a complex issue, he is prone to depend upon his personal leanings as a substitute for law and equity. This situation is compounded by absence of effective control on the judicial conduct by making them accountable. The code of judicial conduct expects judges to uphold the integrity and independence of the judiciary, and avoid impropriety and even appearance of impropriety in all his activities, and perform the duties of his office impartially and diligently which requires enforcement. The problems created by judges who do not understand the law, or irresponsibly handle the matters that they decide or act improperly with prejudice, promote injustice. The remedy for removing this obstacle to justice perhaps lies in handing over the reins of judicial power to persons known for their competence, understanding of law and impartiality. Judicial incompetence and irrationality in decision making process should be detected and dealt with by appropriate judicial reforms aimed at raising the quality of the judicial system.

## Perjury

A dirty little secret of the judicial system that no one wants to admit or confront is perjury towards which the system has turned a blind eye. The fact is, perjury occurs in court cases as a regular feature. People would be shocked if it were truly known how many witnesses lie under oath in courts every day. Lying under oath undermines the very purpose of recording evidence to search for the truth. There is no systematic study of this malaise that hampers justice both in civil and criminal cases. When under oath, a party or witness is under an obligation to tell truth but if he deliberately deviates or an authority prepares a false statement on oath, it is a serious offence and inaction in detecting and dealing with cases of perjury, and fabrication of false evidence has resulted in grave prejudice to the outcome of the proceedings with justice as a casualty defeating interests of the society and encouraging wrongs and crimes. In all cases where the witnesses are proved to be disowning their previous versions recorded by any authority before whom the witness was obliged to tell truth under the law, there should be a compulsory investigation provided under the law to find out whether the previous version was correctly recorded by the officer or authority concerned and action taken against the defaulters.

## Independence and Impartiality

The mandate on the independence of judges and lawyers was established by the UN Commission on Human Rights in 1994 in response to the increasing frequency of attacks on the independence of judges, lawyers and court officers, and link exists between the weakening of safeguards for the judiciary and lawyers and the gravity and frequency of violations of human rights. The special rapporteur in the report to the Commission noted that considerable concerns are beginning to be expressed over judicial corruption, and acknowledged that problems concerning independence and impartiality of judiciary are not confined to the countries or territories noted in the report. In general, the cases and communications summarised in the report *inter alia* referred to the 'taint of corruption and political influence on the judicial system' (see United Nations Commission on Human Rights 56th session 20 March to 28 April, 2000 IV *Thematic Reports* under sub-head 'Independence of Judges and lawyers'). There should not be any *'quid pro quo'* element in making or securing judicial appointments amongst those empowered to initiate the process for such appointments. The usefulness of the incumbent should be for the judicial office that he would hold and not for the possible gains of those who have a voice in such appointments. No appointment to a judicial post should be made on any consideration other than the suitability of the incumbent. The efforts to establish a predictable and effective judicial system are imperative. Judicial reform that ensures the attraction of qualified and efficient individuals into the legal system and greater judicial independence will provide a stronger rule of law.

## Minority Rights and Violence

The Constitutional guarantees to religious minorities, cultural and educational rights, right against exploitation, right to freedom, right to life and personal liberty, empowerment of the state to make special provisions for women and children and for the advancement of any socially and economically backward classes of citizens or for scheduled castes and scheduled tribes, are the built-in safeguards in the legal system which if properly adhered to are capable of reaching the goal of justice for the sectors of the community which may be vulnerable to violence and violations of their rights.

There is much common in the miseries caused by all human rights violations. The mob attacks whether generated by hate against a particular race, or members of a minority community, or a class of people, be it politically motivated, or caused by issue reactions, leave the same impact of devastations on the victims left behind in helpless agony. While it would be ideal to evolve standards and means to prevent violence directed against the vulnerable sectors of the community, the administration of justice is vitally concerned and responsible for providing adequate relief to the victims and to punish the guilty. The post-violence scenario is not merely a matter of law and order. The state has a special role to play in relief and rehabilitation of people affected by arson, loot and violence and to restore sense of security amongst the affected people. For restoration of trust amongst the affected persons irrespective of the sectors of the communities to which they belong, the foremost requirement is to provide adequate protection against violence and swiftly bring to justice the perpetrators of the crimes irrespective of their connections and affiliations. While some advocate setting up of special courts of inquiry or inquiry commissions, it would be appropriate to put the law in motion by swiftly launching the prosecutions, arresting the culprits, collecting evidence and filing charge-sheets in the courts empowered to try such offenders. There is no need to first have elaborate inquiries and let time pass allowing for maneuverings to take place and then launch belated prosecutions after gathering conflicting versions that are often doctored.

There are wide ramifications of mob violence. During mob frenzies, there are horrendous deeds of murder, besieging of houses, acts of *incendiarism* and other scenes of violence in which political witches revel. The wantonness of the inciters and those who thrive on such strife amongst the members of the communities must be detected and severely dealt with to end the vicious circle that is brought about by such criminals to destroy peace and amity.

## Racism, Religious and Political Bigotry

Grave concerns have been expressed at certain manifestations of racism, religious and political bigotry, racial discrimination and related intolerance, and all civilised nations in one voice have condemned the spurt in conflicts arising from the negative aspects of human conduct. Governments attempt at normalisation amongst the various rival parties to such conflicts through democratic norms but the democratic paradox is that even parties which disavow the democratic principles of shunning discriminations on the grounds of caste, creed or religion, seek accession to power through democratic channels by manifestos that discriminate parochial ideologies. The propaganda that divides the community is aimed at gaining political mileage for coming to power, but the monster that is created in the process would destroy every thing that is just and proper. The General Assembly in its resolution 54/153 of 17th December, 1999 concerning measures to combat contemporary forms of racism, racial discrimination, xenophobia and related intolerance, expressed its profound concern about and unequivocal condemnation of all racist violence, including related acts of random and indiscriminate violence, propaganda, activities and organisations based on doctrines of superiority of one race or group of persons that attempt to justify or promote racism and racial discrimination in any form.

At the regional seminar for central and eastern European states, which took place in Warsaw from 5th to 7th July, 2000 in preparation for the World Conference against Racism, experts focussed on the protection of minorities and strengthening human rights capacity at national level. The High Commissioner for Human Rights while opening the seminar said: "The United Nations Declaration on the Rights of Persons Belonging to National or Ethnic,

Religious and Linguistic Minorities, and regional instruments of the OSCE and Council of Europe, have sought to undergird, the legal protection of minorities and vulnerable groups. Their faithful implementation in letter and in spirit, remains a key challenge before us." The protection of minority rights and prevention of ethnic conflicts was also discussed at the October 2000 Regional Seminar of Experts for Africa, held in Addis Ababa, Ethiopia. The seminar encouraged full participation in political life for all, non-discriminatory treatment of all regions and ethnic groups within a country and respect for the rights of minorities. Implementation of the policies for minorities should be done in a manner and with the purpose of bringing about a long-term stability and not just to appease the international community. Providing for the safeguards of the interests of minorities should not just be a strategy for pandering to special interest groups and appearing to be politically correct. There should be a genuine commitment on the part of the state functionaries including the judicial system to protect the identity of national minorities and create conditions for the promotion of that identity.

The General Assembly while considering the report of the Special Rapporteur noted the case of Amadon Diallo, a young Guinean immigrant, who on 4th February, 1999 had died after being shot 41 times by four New York city policemen. The Special Rapporteur noted that four policemen charged with this murder had been acquitted. While refraining from comment on the verdict he observed that "The *Diallo case* is one of more than a dozen incidents, in the past five years, in which black, Hispanic or other minorities have been shot in highly questionable and disputed circumstances", and cited the Presidential comment that Amadon Diallo would not have died had he been living in a white neighbourhood [see A/55/304 Fifty-fifth sessions 'Elimination of racism and racial discrimination, "Report of Special Rapporteur of the Commission on Human Rights on contemporary forms of racism, racial discrimination xenophobia and related intolerance]. This disturbing instance of gross violation of human rights is typical of happenings during the period of violent disturbances that occur because of religious and racial intolerance, and the miseries caused by the fellowmen are compounded by the guardians of law and order. Then where does the sufferer look, to get succor and speedy justice. This brings into sharp focus the need to remove obstructions in the way of the victims of intolerance and highhandedness in securing judicial justice.

## Police Brutalities

The superior courts in India are armed with powers strong enough to direct the executive for failing in its duties to discharge them. On being seized of the complaint about deliberate failures and lapses of the executive and the police force it controls, can be dealt with, by issuing appropriate directions to the authorities to take action against the culprits by arrest and prosecution, and to provide security to the victims or potential victims of the frenzy. In cases of police brutality and atrocities committed in utter disregard and in all breaches of human rights and constitutional guarantees, the Supreme Court of India is committed to uphold human rights even as a part of long standing heritage and as enshrined in the Constitutional Law of India. Courts have frequently dealt with cases of brutality practised by overzealous police officers who resort to inhuman and barbaric ways of treating the suspects while collecting evidence and in dealing with instances of custodial deaths caused during interrogations and other investigations. The Supreme Court of India on several occasions has awarded exemplary compensation to the victims at the hands of the police officials (see *Kartar Singh V. State of Punjab (1994) 3 SCC 569)*. No one should be subjected to physical violence of person or torture of any kind which undermines the faith of the community in the efficacy of criminal justice system. In a case where the Supreme Court made a reference to the National Human Rights Commission to have the matter of unceremonious disposal of thousands of dead bodies by the police examined and jurisdiction of the Commission was questioned with reference to its statutory obligations and period of limitation for enquiry as provided under Section 36(2) of the Protection of Human Rights Act, 1993, the Supreme Court held that the Commission is a body *sui juris* created under the Act made by Parliament for examining and investigating the questions and complaints relating to violation of human rights, as also the negligence on the part of any public servant in preventing such violations. It was held that when the Supreme Court, in exercise of the jurisdiction under Article 32 of the Constitution, entrusted the Commission with the task of getting the matter examined, the Commission in doing so would function pursuant to the directions of the Supreme Court which were binding on all authorities in India and in deciding the matters so referred the Commission had a free hand and was not circumscribed by any conditions. The jurisdiction exercised by the Commission at the behest of the Supreme Court was of a special nature not covered by any enactment or law. The bar contained in section 36(2) which prescribed a period of limitation was held not to apply in such a situation (see *Paramjit Kaur V. State of Punjab (1999)2 SCC 131)*.

## XII. Immunity as a Defence

The above approach of the Supreme Court assumes greater significance in context of the defence of immunity often put up by the police officers or the government. No one can demand absolute immunity or claim unquestionable right and unlimited powers that disregard basic human rights. In context of the provisions of sections 159 and 160 of the Bombay Police Act, 1951, affording an absolute immunity to a public servant from any penalty or liability to pay damages in respect of any 'act done in good faith' in pursuance of or intended in pursuance of "any duty imposed or any authority conferred on him by any provision of this Act or any other law for the time being in force or any rule, order or direction made or given thereunder." It has been held by the apex court that such absolute immunity is not afforded in respect of any offence or wrong alleged to have been done by a public servant, if it was done under colour or in access of any such duty or authority (see *K.K.Patel V. State of Gujarat (2000) 6SCC 195*). It may be necessary in the wake of terrorists activities, communal riots or mob violence to deal with the situation firmly which may require sufficient empowerment of the police officers and paramilitary forces so as not to wait till they are shot at, but administrative liquidation is certainly not a course open to them. Thus, in a case where two persons along with some others were just apprehended from a hut, taken to a long distance away and shot dead there by the police, the Supreme Court of India held that this type of activity cannot be countenanced by the courts even in the case of disturbed areas (*People's Union for Civil Liberties V. Union of India (1997) 3 SCC 433* ). The defence of sovereign immunity is inapplicable, and alien to the concept of guarantee of fundamental rights. Immunity should not be allowed to remain an obstacle to justice in cases of police excesses and atrocities. Not only is it within court's power to overcome such obstacles but the court also has an obligation to grant relief to the victim or the heir of the victim by directing the state to pay suitable compensation for the damage caused by its officers by violating the fundamental rights of the citizen. It is a sound policy to punish the wrongdoer and it is in that spirit that

tion or do a poor job in presenting a case. There are many reaso. why prosecutors may choose not to pursue a case against an allegedly brutal police officer. The traditionally close association between the public prosecutors and police officers who usually work together prosecuting criminals, militates against vigorous pursuit of cases of police excesses. Special procedural protections for public officials including police officers accused of criminal conduct make criminal indictment difficult. These factors embolden officers committing human rights violations as they have little reason to fear successful prosecution. There should 'therefore' be created a special prosecutor's office to handle criminal prosecutions of officers accused of human rights violations including cases of brutality and corruption. Barriers to the filing of complaints should be removed and under no circumstances should the intake officer attempt to dissuade or intimidate the complainants. Any officer who attempts to dissuade a complainant from filing a complaint should be appropriately punished. Governments and law enforcement agencies should ensure that superior officers are held responsible if they know, or should have known that law enforcement officials under their command are resorting, or have resorted to the unlawful use of force and firearms, and they did not take all measures at their command to prevent, suppress or report such use (see U.N. Basic Principles on the use of Force and Firearms by Law Enforcement Officials which call for accountability for superior Officers - *Principle 24 UN DOC A/CONE.144/28/Rev./(1990))*.

## Poverty

Extreme poverty is a denial of all human rights. Within the framework of the United Nations Decade for the Eradication of Poverty (1997-2006), the General Assembly has set itself two distinct goals: to eradicate absolute poverty and to reduce substantially overall poverty in the world (*Resolution 53/198*). An individual in a situation of poverty still has a possibility of exercising certain rights, whereas extreme poverty implies a total lack of resources and means of social integration (see *report of A..M.Lizin, Independent Expert E/CN.4/2000/52, 25th 'February' 2000 para 12*). The extremely poor cannot express themselves or play any role in the communities in which they live. They lack resources for livelihood and have no means to approach or even reach the court. Having no means to bear any expense for transport, such person will be forced to walk to reach the court if summoned. The first priority would 'therefore' be to combat extreme poverty that is the biggest obstacle to justice. The violent clashes in the communities, armed conflicts and natural disasters have devastating effects that may generate extreme poverty. Extreme poverty continues to spread in all countries of the world. The gulf between the rich and those living in dire poverty is widening. The rich may adopt a 'fortress mentality' to defend their prosperity against perceived external threats and exploit migrants and displaced persons who provide cheap labour. The simmering discontentment can explode into a riotous situation. The fortress mentality is assuming global dimensions and the international community faces a fundamental choice "either we envisage a world of two vastly different parts, one with ever increasing wealth and technological sophistication, the other a place where people live in abject poverty; or we embrace the idea that we are all in this together as members of one human family, with entitlements to economic, social and cultural rights which need to be progressively implemented. This embracing option regards diversity as strength, not weakness, and recognises the great social, cultural, and yes, economic benefits of a multicultural society. It is a vision of a world where people of all colours, creeds and standing live together in harmony and peace" (address by Mary Robinson, United Nations High Commissioner for Human Rights and Secretary General of the World Conference against Racism on 1st May, 2000.)

The poor lack the information about the programs of ameliorating their plight. Every law enacted, particularly welfare legislation for the benefit of the poor must be implemented in the proper spirit for achieving the noble object for which such law is made. It becomes the duty of the court to ensure that rehabilitation measures contained in the legislative provisions are properly implemented. The fundamental rights to life and against exploitation cast a duty on the government to suitably rehabilitate bonded labourers freed but living in a State of abject poverty (*see Neeraja Chaudhary V. State of MP (1984) 3 SCC 243* ). Social backwardness is, on ultimate analysis, the result of poverty to a very large extent. Poverty demands affirmative action and its eradication is a constitutional mandate. The Supreme Court of India has observed that in final analysis, poverty which is the ultimate result of inequities and which is the immediate cause and effect of backwardness has to be eradicated not merely by reservation policy, but by free medical aid, free elementary education, scholarships for higher education and other financial support, free housing, self-employment and settlement schemes, effective implementation of land reforms, strict and impartial operation of law-enforcing machinery... free water supply.. and other ameliorative measures particularly in the areas densely populated by backward classes of citizens. (*see Indra Sawhney V. Union of India 1992 supp (3) SCC 217*). Free legal assistance at State cost is considered to be a fundamental right of a person accused of an offence which may jeopardize his life or personal liberty and this fundamental right is held to be implicit in the requirement of reasonable, fair and just procedure. The exercise of this fundamental right does not depend upon the accused applying for legal aid and even if the accused failed to apply he is entitled to legal aid. The Supreme Court of India has held that it would be the mockery of the legal aid programme if it were to be left to the poor, ignorant and illiterate accused to ask for free legal services (see *Suk Das V. Union Territory of Arunachal Pradesh, (1986) 2 SCC 401* ). Article 39A of The Constitution of India provides that the state shall secure that the operation of the legal system promotes justice, on a basis of equal opportunity, and shall, in particular, provide free legal aid, by suitable legislation or schemes or in any other way, to ensure that the opportunities for securing justice are not denied to any citizen by reason of economic or other disabilities. The Parliament has framed *Legal Services Authorities Act, 1987* to *inter alia* constitute legal services authorities to provide free and competent legal services to the weaker sectors of the society to ensure that opportunities for securing justice are not denied to any citizen by reason of economic or other disabilities. The elaborate provisions of the Act have been operating successfully to obviate obstacles in the way of the poor by providing them free and competent access to justice.

## Internally Displaced Persons

(1) Internal displacement of persons may be caused due to various reasons. It may be caused by natural calamities like earthquakes, submergence or mass exodus from one locality or area to the other, due to violence or other compulsions. The guiding principles on Internal Displacement (see E/CN.4/1998/53/ Add.2) set out the rights and guarantees under the international law relevant to the protection of internally displaced persons in all phases of displacement. The principles affirm that the responsibilities for ensuring the protection of internally displaced persons rest primarily with the national authorities. A

proper information about internally displaced persons can help in providing emergency relief promptly and to speed up efforts to assist and protect them. The internally displaced persons have to be rehabilitated. Rehabilitation is not mere providing of shelter. The real purpose of rehabilitation can be achieved only if those who are sought to be rehabilitated are provided with shelter, food and other necessary amenities of life. Thus, allotment of land to provide a hospital for the disabled and for the crippled children of displaced persons was held by the Supreme Court of India to squarely come within the concept of the idea of 'rehabilitation' and consequently settlement of the refugees, (see Collector of 24 Paragnas V. Lalit Mohan Mullick, (1986) 2 SCC 138).

Trends in human population movements due to industrialisation, lack of protection in workplace and passions whipped up by the political or religious leaders can result in domestic violence which has to be guarded against by regulation of public health, housing, employment, and education, and adequate security and above all access to justice. The fact that court can take innovative steps to speed up rehabilitation of citizens displaced due to natural calamity of a devastating earthquake that erased all buildings to ground in many towns and villages of Kachchh is evident from a recent decision of the High Court of Gujarat in which the court holding that the donations and contributions in cash and kind received for helping the earthquake victims were held in trust by the government and that the funds were to be subject to periodic audit to ensure proper utilisation, ordered the District Judge cum District Chairman of Legal Services Authority to act as Ombudsman in the work of distribution of relief materials in cash and kind to the quake victims and to redress their grievances and ensure that the citizens were not maltreated (see *Bipinchandra J. Divan & ors. V. State of Gujarat & ors. , 2001 (2) GLR 1395* ).

## Conclusions

The concern of the international community to deal with the obstacles to access to justice is justified because the oppressed and the wronged who are denied justice may resort to revolt and violence or helplessly face extinction. The primary concern of the nations should be to remove the internal obstacles to access to justice which lie under the cover of power in the hidden forms of lack of understanding the law, inability to deal with cases, prejudices, amenability to political and other influences, the taint of corruption and insensitivity to human sufferings. The other obstructions hampering access to justice in the delicate areas of human relationship and peaceful co-existence which disturb the very fabric of a multicultural society are racial and religious intolerance, mob violence, extreme poverty, flaws in the legal system, propaganda of hatred, police brutalities, and they call for a concerted effort of an enlightened judicial system and the governance that interest of all the citizens to its heart be saved without searching for cleavages providing ropeways for journey to power. The neglect in removing obstacles to access to justice is fraught with grave dangers that may perpetuate strife and miseries thwart all progress and encourage mercenary activities giving rise to criminal acts of a terrorist nature. The solutions are there waiting for the will of the state functionaries to bring peace, harmony and prosperity.

To conclude, it is evident that globally people are unable to get their Human Rights, what they are getting is the Discriminatory Human Rights, Deprivatory Human Rights, or Differential Human Rights. Judiciary, Human Rights activists, academicians policy makers are expected to work together to provide equal Human Rights to all Human Beings without any consideration of Caste, religion. creed, gender, social categories, considerations. am sure a day will come in Human History when each Human being will have uniform Human Rights.

In India, the human rights commission at the state level are yet to function independently. The interference of state government is visible and in some state rules are yet to be framed. Let the union government of India grant uniformity in rules and regulation of state human rights commission and allow to function for the common man. Further, it has emerged from field data that the IPS and IAS must not be appointed either full time or part time in the human rights commission as they worked for breaking/depriving human rights of the common and suddenly they become protector of human rights which is not possible for them because their long attitude to human rights continue even after joining human rights commission.

# Index